CROSS STITCH

CROSS STITCH

OVER 70 STUNNING PROJECTS TO TEMPT YOU

MURDOCH BOOKS®

Sydney • London • Vancouver • New York

CONTENTS

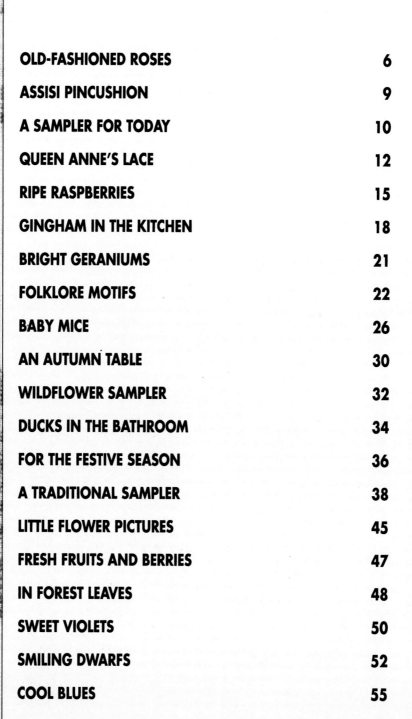

CONTENTS

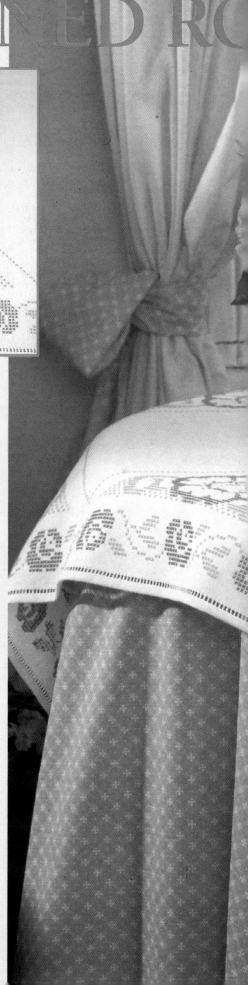

SUITABLE FOR BEGINNERS

The rose is perhaps the most loved of all flowers — and no wonder, when it brings so much pleasure. The charming square tablecloth is made from hardanger fabric. The border is decorated with small roses. For the large roses in the centre, simply fill in the background and the shape of the motifs will appear. Embroider these lovely shelf borders, too: make wide borders with large roses, or narrow borders with smaller ones.

TABLECLOTH

Materials

88 cm square piece of white hardanger fabric with 9 double fabric threads to 1 cm
DMC stranded embroidery cottons in cranberry pink number 603, Nile green number 954, and light turquoise number 598

Finished size About 85 cm square. The graph is on foldout sheet A. See the General Instructions and Stitch Library on pages 92–6.

Method Following the graph, embroider the motifs on the hardanger fabric. Work in cross stitch over two double fabric threads using two strands of cotton. Start the embroidery in the right lower corner at A, 9 cm from the fabric edges. Leave a space of one double fabric thread between each cross, lengthways and widthways. Repeat the centre section (exactly one-quarter of the cloth) three more times.

When completed, embroider the border of roses around the cloth: the green stems and leaves face the same direction on each edge of the cloth.

To finish Baste a 7.5 mm double hem around the cloth. Withdraw three double fabric threads above the hem up to the corners where these threads intersect. Weave the short ends of the threads back into the fabric corners. Sew the hem in place by working ladder hemstitch over three double fabric threads, using one strand of cotton to match the fabric.

SHELF BORDERS

Materials

5 cm or 8 cm wide strip of hardanger fabric with 9 double fabric threads to 1 cm, in the desired length plus at least 2 cm for turnings
DMC stranded embroidery cottons in cranberry pink number 603 and Nile green number 954

Finished size Width of borders 3 cm or 6 cm.
The graph is on foldout sheet A.

See the General Instructions and Stitch Library on pages 92–6.

Method Following the graph for the tablecloth, embroider the rose border in the centre of the band. Work in cross stitch over two double fabric threads, using two strands of embroidery cotton. For the wide band, always leave a space of one double fabric thread between each cross, lengthways as well as widthways. Repeat the motif for the required length. For the narrow band, follow the graph but do not allow extra spaces. Finish the raw edges of the band with narrow hems. (1 cm hem allowance on each side.)

ASSISI PINCUSHION

PINCUSHION

Materials

12 x 24 cm piece of pale pink linen 11
DMC stranded embroidery cottons, dark red 498 and dusty rose 961
35 cm pink cord
Synthetic fibrefill or wool scraps

Finished size 8.5 cm square.
See the General Instructions and Stitch Library on pages 92–6.

Method Cut the linen into two 12 cm squares. Following the graph, embroider the large motif on one piece of linen. Work in cross stitch over two fabric threads, using two strands of embroidery cotton. Start the embroidery at M, in the centre and 2 cm from the lower edge. To complete the motif, repeat it three more times. When the cross stitching is complete, embroider the four-sided stitches using number 498. Following the graph, embroider the small star motif in the centre of the remaining piece of linen.

To finish Cut each embroidered piece into an 11 x 11 cm octagon (i.e. 1.25 cm away from the four-sided stitches). With *wrong sides* facing, and a 1 cm wide seam allowance turned to the wrong side, sew the pieces together, filling the pincushion while sewing. (Scraps of wool from knitting or embroidery are the best filling for pincushions, as the small amount of natural oil remaining in the yarn helps prevent pins rusting.) Sew a piece of cord on top of the seam.

A star motif is worked in simple Assisi embroidery on this pincushion. In Assisi work, the design is left open, and the background is filled in with crosses. If you have never tried this cross stitch technique, a pincushion is the perfect introduction. To complete the piece, a simple star shape is worked on the back of the cushion.

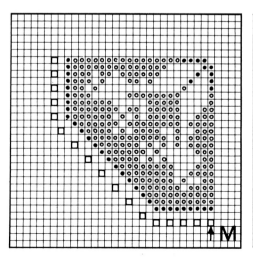

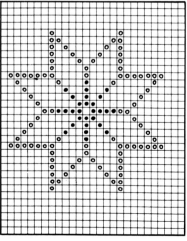

Colour key for the pincushion

	Colour	DMC
●	Dark red	498
◎	Dusty rose	961

ABCDEFGHIJKLMNOPQRSTUVW
abcdefghijklmnopqrstuvwxyz ABCDEF
NOPQRSTUVWXYZ
12
ABCDEFGHIJKLMNO
E M
M B F M

A SAMPLER FOR TODAY

A modern interpretation of the traditional sampler, this lovely piece is made in fine linen and embroidered in pale tones of blue, green, yellow and brown. It reproduces many favourite old motifs, such as the basket and vases of flowers. Many motifs have a deeper meaning: the trees, for instance, symbolise life and freedom. And, as always, there are alphabets in different styles.

SAMPLER

Materials

50 x 55 cm piece of ecru linen 12
DMC stranded embroidery cottons
in the colours indicated on the
colour key on foldout sheet D

Method Following the graph, embroider the motifs on the linen. Work in cross stitch over two fabric threads, using two strands of embroidery cotton. Start the embroidery at the lower right corner, 10 cm in from the edges. Work the eyes of the figures at the base in french knots using medium brown number 433.

To finish Finish the completed embroidery with an openwork hem, or frame it as desired.

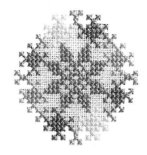

Finished size Embroidered area is 28 x 35 cm.
The graph is on foldout sheet D.
See the General Instructions and Stitch Library on pages 92–6.

UEEN ANNE'S LACE

Queen Anne's lace is a pretty, delicate plant with small white flowers—not only special in the garden, but also beautiful when embroidered in cross stitch on a wall hanging. The linen background is first shaded with fabric dye. The unusual effect is obtained by is gradually dying the background from dark to lighter blue. The book cover is embroidered in petit point on fine linen, dyed an even blue.

WALL HANGING

Materials

85 x 125 cm white linen 8
DMC stranded embroidery cottons in the colours indicated on the colour key on foldout sheet E
Textile dye, such as Dylon hot water dye, colour number 18

Finished size Embroidered area measures about 48 x 74 cm.
The graph is on foldout sheet E.
See the General Instructions and Stitch Library on pages 92–6.

Dyeing Following the instructions on the package of the textile paint, dye a few small test pieces of white linen first. Experiment to obtain the desired colour; only a very small amount of dye is needed to obtain a pale tone.

To dye the actual piece of linen, remove the top part quickly from the dye pot, the middle section a bit later, and keep the lower section in the longest. During dyeing, move the fabric gently to and fro to obtain a shaded effect. Dry the fabric, and iron.

Embroidery Following the graph, embroider the motif in cross stitch. Work the crosses over two fabric threads, using four strands of embroidery cotton. Start the embroidery at the right lower corner, 30 cm from the right edge (one long side) and 20 cm from the lower edge (one short side). When all cross stitching is complete, work the outlines in back-stitch, using two strands of cotton.

To finish Finish the embroidery with an openwork hem, or frame it as desired.

BOOKCOVER

Materials

A book
A piece of white linen 12
measuring: the height of the book
plus 10 cm, and as wide as the
width of the front, spine and back
of the book, plus about 25 cm
DMC stranded embroidery cottons
in the colours indicated on the
colour key and also dark Delft blue
number 798
Textile dye, such as hot-water dye
Dylon colour number 18
Lining
A piece of light blue fabric the
same size as the linen

Finished size Embroidered area
measures 15 x 25 cm.
The graph is on foldout sheet E.
See the General Instructions and Stitch
Library on pages 92–6.

Dyeing Following the instructions on
the package of the textile dye, dye a few
small test pieces of white linen first.
Experiment to obtain the desired colour.
Only a very small amount of dye is
needed to obtain a pale tone. Dye the
piece of linen. Dry and iron the linen.

Embroidery Place the linen around
the book and decide on the placement of
the motif on the front of the cover.
Following the graph, embroider the
motif in continental stitch. Work each
stitch (half cross) over one fabric thread
using two strands of embroidery cotton.
Each stitch will lie diagonally over two
fabric threads at the back (see the Stitch
Library).When all continental stitching
is completed, work the outlines in
backstitch, using one strand of cotton.
Start the embroidery at the right lower
corner. Trace the flower name onto
tracing paper, and using textile carbon
or a pencil, copy it below the plant.

Embroider the name with number 798
using one strand of cotton.

To finish Cut the embroidered
piece to fit the book, adding a 1 cm
wide seam allowance at the top and

lower edges, and 7 cm each at the side
edges. With right sides facing, stitch
the embroidered piece and the lining
together, making a 1 cm wide seam,
and leaving a small opening on one of
the side seams for turning. Cut corners
diagonally, turn through, and slipstitch
the opening closed. Fold both short
sides 6 cm towards the middle and
hand sew in place along the top and
bottom edges. Finally, slip the book
inside the cover.

Queen Anne's Lace

RIPE RASPBERRIES

ake this festive cloth for a summery table. The panel of juicy raspberries runs along the centre of the cloth, so it can be clearly seen and admired, even when the table is fully laid. Matching serviettes, made from a small piece of linen, have an openwork hem. And, to complete the setting, the attractive matching serviette rings can be made very quickly from a small piece of linen. The pretty pink linen gives a most delicate appearance.

TABLECLOTH

Materials

1.90 m of 140 cm wide pale pink linen 10
DMC stranded embroidery cottons in the colours indicated on the colour key, plus medium grey-green number 3052, and deep canary yellow number 973

Finished size Tablecloth 125 x 170 cm. The graph is on foldout sheet A.
See the General Instructions and Stitch Library on pages 92–6.

Method Following the graph, embroider the motif on the linen. Work in cross stitch over two fabric threads, using two strands of embroidery cotton. Start the embroidery at A, in the centre of one short side, and 11.5 cm inside the edge. Repeat the motif eight more times, omitting the section at the left of line B–C for the last repeat. When the cross stitching is complete, work the outlines in backstitch using two strands of embroidery cotton. Work the stamens in straight stitch and a french knot using two strands of cotton.

When the embroidery is complete, work one row of four-sided stitch along the outer edge of the cloth, 9 cm from the edges. Work the stitches over three fabric threads using two strands of light carnation number 893.

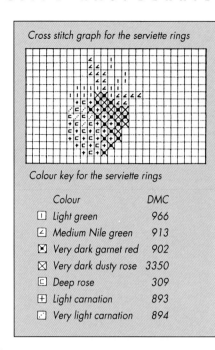

Cross stitch graph for the serviette rings

Colour key for the serviette rings

	Colour	DMC
☐	Light green	966
◿	Medium Nile green	913
⊠	Very dark garnet red	902
⊠	Very dark dusty rose	3350
◖	Deep rose	309
⊞	Light carnation	893
⬚	Very light carnation	894

To finish Baste a 3 cm wide double hem around the cloth. Mitre the corners. Secure the hem at the back along the row of four-sided stitch.

SERVIETTES

Materials

For one serviette
44 cm square piece of pale pink linen 10
Small quantity of DMC stranded embroidery cotton in light carnation number 893

Finished size About 40 cm square. See the General Instructions and Stitch Library on pages 92–6.

Method Baste a 1 cm wide double hem all around the linen. Make mitred corners. Withdraw four fabric threads above the hem from corner to corner where these threads intersect. Weave the short ends of the threads back into the fabric. Secure the hem with open hemstitch worked over five fabric threads, using one strand of embroidery cotton.

SERVIETTE RINGS

Materials

For one serviette ring
6.5 x 17 cm piece of pale pink linen 10
DMC stranded embroidery cottons in the colours indicated on the colour key
Lining 4.5 x 15 cm piece of pale pink linen
A small button

Finished size 4.5 x 15 cm.
See the General Instructions and Stitch Library on pages 92–6.

Method Following the graph on page 16, embroider the raspberry motif in the centre of the linen. Work in cross stitch over two fabric threads using two strands of embroidery cotton. Position the lower edge of the raspberry on the long side of the fabric.

To finish Along one short side and two long sides, work one row of four-sided edge stitch (see Stitch Library). Position the row 1 cm from the edges. Work the stitches over four fabric threads using two strands of light carnation number 893.

With *wrong sides* together, place the lining fabric against the back of the embroidered piece. Turn under 1 cm of linen, that is, along the top edge of the row of four-sided edge stitches, over the outer edges of the lining piece. Working through all fabric layers, secure the turning with four-sided edge stitch (see Stitch Library). Cut away any surplus fabric at the back.

Make a buttonhole loop on the short side with the embroidered edging. Neaten the opposite short side and sew the button in the corresponding spot.

GINGHAM IN THE K

Brighten up your kitchen with this cheerful border embroidered in two colours. It is easy to work and the result is worth the effort. Combine the border with brightly coloured gingham to make an attractive apron or curtain. The border also looks pretty on a cupboard shelf. Whatever colour gingham you want to use, the colour of the flower can be altered to match.

CAFÉ CURTAINS

Materials

For one curtain Red and white gingham measuring about 75 cm long (height) and the width of window 8 cm wide piece of white hardanger fabric with 9 double fabric threads to 1 cm as long as the width of the curtain plus at least 2 cm for turnings
DMC stranded embroidery cottons in the colours in the colour key

Finished size Length (height) about 55 cm.
See the General Instructions and Stitch Library on pages 92–6.

Method Following graph, embroider motif in cross stitch in centre of hardanger band. Work each cross over two double fabric threads, with two strands of embroidery cotton. Repeat motif for desired length.

To finish Make a 5 cm wide hem, with 2 cm turned under, along the lower edge. With the wrong side of the band against the right side of the curtain, stitch the band onto the curtain, with raw edges turned to the wrong side (1 cm seam allowances on each edge) about 3 cm from the lower side. Make a narrow hem along the sides of the curtain. Make a 6 cm wide casing, with 5 cm turned under, along the top edge. Insert a rod for hanging the curtain. Make a second curtain in the same way.

SHELF BORDER

Materials

8 cm wide piece of white hardanger fabric with 9 double fabric threads to 1 cm in the length desired, plus at least 2 cm for turnings

DMC stranded embroidery cottons in the colours indicated on the colour key

Finished size Width of border about 6 cm.

See the General Instructions and Stitch Library on pages 92–6.

Method Following graph, embroider motif in cross stitch in centre of hardanger band. Work each cross over two double fabric threads, using two strands of embroidery cotton. Repeat motif for required length. Finish raw edges of band with a narrow hem (1 cm seam allowance included on all edges). Use craft glue sparingly to attach border to shelf.

APRON

Materials

90 cm of 120 cm wide red and white gingham

3.50 m green bias binding

8 x 35 cm piece of white hardanger fabric with 9 double fabric threads to 1 cm

DMC stranded embroidery cottons in the colours indicated on the colour key

Finished size About 85 cm long (without ties)

See the General Instructions and Stitch Library on pages 92–6.

Method Following the graph, embroider the motif in cross stitch. Work each cross over two double fabric threads, using two strands of embroidery cotton. Start the embroidery at M, in the centre of the band. Embroider one more motif on each side of the centre motif.

Enlarge the pattern graph for the apron and cut out the paper pattern. Cut the pattern from the fabric without a seam allowance, but add a 1 cm wide seam allowance on the top edge. For the facing, cut one strip 8 x 29 cm; for the neck tie, one strip 6 x 63 cm; and for the ties, two strips 8 x 65 cm.

Assembly Press the neck tie in half across its width. With right sides together and the short ends of the neck tie inserted between, stitch the facing along the top edge of the apron: keep all raw edges even, and ensure that the raw edges of the tie are aligned with the side edges of the apron. Fold the facing inwards and sew the lower edge in place with a turning. With the wrong side of the embroidered band against the right side of the apron and all raw edges turned under (1 cm seam allowances), stitch the embroidered band to the apron. Position the embroidery about 3 cm from the top edge. Cut the sides of the band even with the sides of the apron. Stitch, in one continuous line, the bias binding along the armholes of the apron and the raw edges of the neck tie. Then finish the lower edge and sides with bias binding, turning in the raw edges at the top. With right sides together, sew the ties in half across their width. Stitch one short side and turn the ties through. Stitch the ties to the inside of the apron with a small turning to the wrong side.

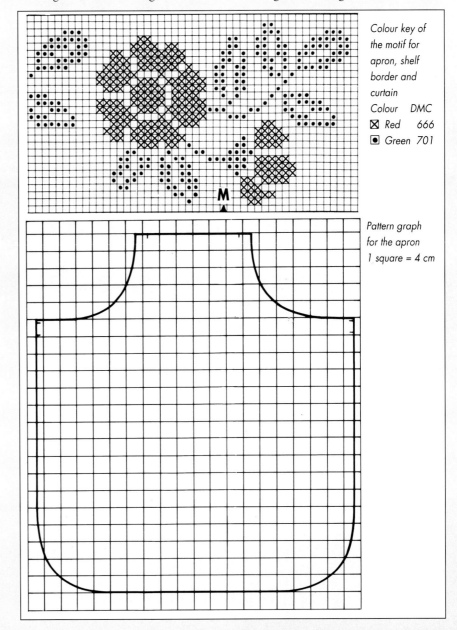

Colour key of the motif for apron, shelf border and curtain

Colour   DMC
☒ Red   666
⬤ Green   701

Pattern graph for the apron
1 square = 4 cm

BRIGHT GERANIUMS

SUITABLE FOR BEGINNERS

*P*ink and red geraniums in terracotta pots brighten these pretty, square cushions. They are made in large-weave Aida-style fabric and can be quickly worked. The design is framed with a border in the colour of one of the flowers.

Materials

For one cushion
One 42 cm square piece of white Hertarette fabric (3 fabric squares to 1 centimetre)(DMC article number 3707)
Lining A 42 cm square piece of white cotton fabric
DMC stranded embroidery cottons in pink, red, green, brown, and dark brown shades of your choice
A 40 cm square cushion insert

Finished size 40 cm square.
See the General Instructions and Stitch Library on pages 92–6.

Method Following the graph, embroider the motifs on the Aida fabric. Work in cross stitch over two fabric squares, using four strands of embroidery cotton. Start the embroidery with the bottom row of the right flower pot, 8 cm from the right edge and 6 cm from the lower edge. For a second cushion, alternate the colours for the flowers, making the red flower at the right side and the pink flower at the left side. Following the small graph, embroider a 36 cm square border around the design, using either red or pink.

To finish Sew the front and back together with right sides facing, leaving a space large enough on one side to insert cushion, but sew around all corners. Use a 1 cm wide seam. Cut the seam corners diagonally and turn the cover through. Place the insert inside the cover and slipstitch the opening closed.

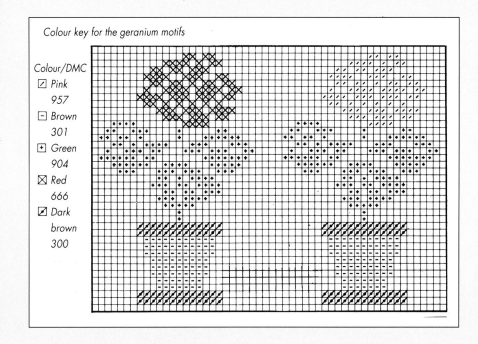

Colour key for the geranium motifs

Colour/DMC
☑ Pink 957
⊟ Brown 301
⊞ Green 904
⊠ Red 666
☑ Dark brown 300

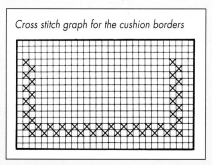

Cross stitch graph for the cushion borders

FOLKLORE MOTIFS

*F*olklore motifs are always charming. Here we have selected a bird and flowers with heart-shaped petals, and used them to adorn a sewing basket, pincushion and small tablecloth.

TABLECLOTH

Materials

75 cm square piece of white linen 12
DMC stranded embroidery cottons in the colours indicated on the colour key

Finished size 67 cm square.
See the General Instructions and Stitch Library on pages 92–6.

Method Make one vertical and one horizontal line in running stitches to indicate the centre of the cloth. Following the graph, embroider the motif in cross stitch. Work each cross over three fabric threads, using two strands of embroidery cotton. Start the embroidery at M, 339 fabric threads away from the centre. Complete the motif. Repeat the motif one more time and then embroider the corner motif. After the corner motif, embroider the motif four times up to the corner. Embroider the corner. Complete the border.

To finish Cut the cloth into a 71 cm square. Baste a 1 cm wide double hem around the cloth, making mitred corners. Above the hem, remove four fabric threads to the corners. Darn the short ends of the threads back into the fabric. Secure the hem with open hemstitch worked over four fabric threads.

SEWING BASKET

Materials

25 x 33 cm piece of white linen 12
DMC stranded embroidery cottons in the colours indicated on the colour key
Extra skein of DMC medium dusty rose number 962 for cord edging
Two pieces 18.5 x 26.5 cm of thin flannelette
18.5 x 26.5 cm piece of synthetic batting

Finished size Lid of basket 19.5 x 27.5 cm.
See the General Instructions and Stitch Library on pages 92–6.

Note Adapt the measurements given if you are using a sewing basket with a different-sized lid.

Method Following the graph, embroider the motif in cross stitch. Work each cross over three fabric threads, using two strands of embroidery cotton. Work the blue border first: start at the right lower corner of one long side, 3 cm from the edges. To complete the design, reverse the motif at M.

To finish Cut the embroidered piece 2 cm away from the blue border. Place the flannel pieces together with a layer of wadding between, and sew this onto the lid of the basket. Sew the embroidery, with 1 cm turned under, on top. Twist a cord from medium dusty rose embroidery cotton number 962 and sew it along the outer edges.

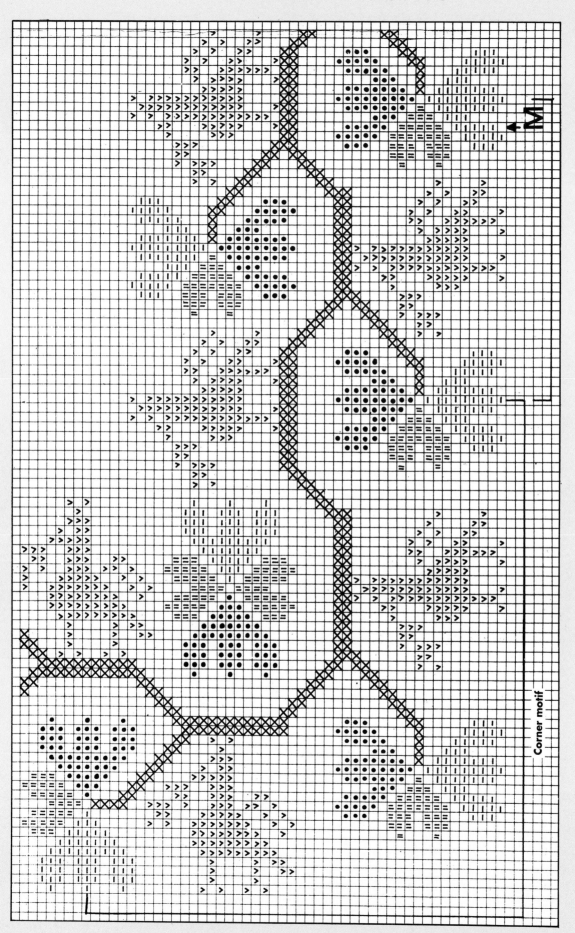

Graph for tablecloth

Clour key for tablecloth, pincushion and basket

⊠	320
⦿	221
�🅸	962
⊟	224
⌄	809

Corner motif

PINCUSHION

Materials

13.5 x 34 cm piece white linen 12
DMC stranded embroidery cottons
in the colours indicated on the
colour key
Synthetic fibrefill or wool scraps

Finished size 11.5 x 13 cm.
See the General Instructions and Stitch
Library on pages 92–6.

Method Cut the linen into two 15
x 17 cm pieces. Following the graph for
the sewing basket, embroider the motif

on one piece of fabric. Work in cross
stitch over three fabric threads, using
two strands of embroidery cotton. Start
the embroidery 2.75 cm from the right
edge and 4 cm from the lower edge
(one short side). Repeat the motif on
the other short side; position the motifs
three fabric threads apart. If necessary,
refer to the photograph of the
completed project. Embroider a frame
of crosses around the motif, placed
twelve fabric threads away from the
embroidery, and work the crosses
nine fabric threads apart. Cut away
surplus fabric about 2 cm away
from border, to make a piece about
13.5 x 15 cm (includes seam

allowances), and cut a second piece the
same size.

To finish With right sides together,
and making a 1 cm wide seam, sew the
pieces together, leaving a small opening
for turning. Turn through and insert the
filling. (Wool scraps from knitting or
embroidery are the perfect filling for
pincushions, as the small amount of oil
remaining in the yarn helps prevent
pins rusting.) Slipstitch the opening
closed.

Graph for sewing basket and pincushion

Motif for pincushion

BABY MICE

TOWELLING JACKET

Materials

A white towelling jacket or singlet
7 cm square of 14 count waste
canvas (14 stitches to 1 inch)
DMC stranded embroidery cottons
in the colours indicated on the
colour key

Finished size Embroidery measures
3.5 x 4.5 cm.
See the General Instructions and Stitch
Library on pages 92–6.

Method Baste the waste canvas onto
the front of the jacket; position it in the
centre, with the top edge 5 cm below the
neckline. Following the graph, embroider
one of the mice in cross stitch. Work
each cross over two fabric thread,
through both layers, using two strands of
embroidery cotton. Keep the needle
perpendicular to the canvas while
working, and stitch only through the
canvas holes, not the canvas threads.
When the cross stitching is complete,
work the outlines in backstitch, using
pewter grey number 317. Dampen the
canvas and remove the basting and the
canvas threads one by one with tweezers.

These friendly mice look endearing on a
whole collection of baby items. There is a bib,
worked on Aida and edged with bias binding, an
Aida band on a striped sheet, a towelling jacket
and a cotton coverall finished with bias binding. The little mice
go hand-in-hand, but the mouse on the bib sits ready at the table.
Lovely gifts for a new baby.

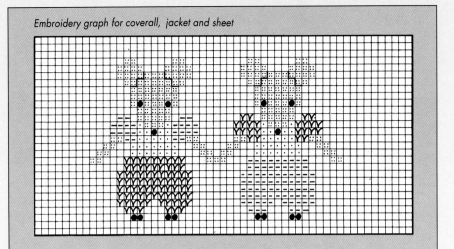

Embroidery graph for coverall, jacket and sheet

BIB

Materials

18 x 20 cm piece of 11 count white Aida fabric
Lining 18 x 20 cm piece of white cotton fabric
DMC stranded embroidery cottons in the colours indicated on the colour key
1.10 m pale green bias binding

Finished size Bib 16 x 18 cm, embroidery 5.5 x 10 cm.
See the General Instructions and Stitch Library on pages 92–6.

Method Enlarge the pattern graph and cut out the paper pattern. Outline the pattern on the fabric with running stitches. Following the graph, embroider the motif in cross stitch. Start the embroidery 3.5 cm from the lower edge, matching M with the centre of the fabric. Work each cross over one fabric square, using two strands of embroidery cotton. When the cross stitching is complete, work the outlines in backstitch, using pewter grey number 317.

To finish Baste the lining fabric against the back of the embroidered piece. Cut the bib on the marked outline. Finish the outer edge with bias binding. Finish the neck edge with bias binding, extending it about 20 cm at each side to form ties.

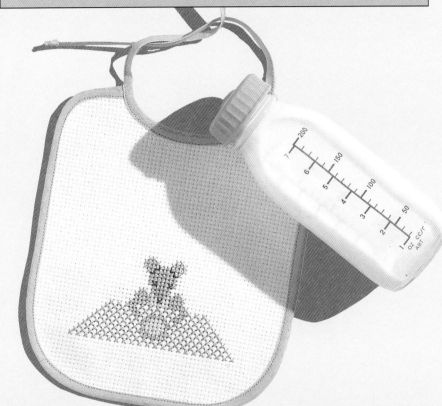

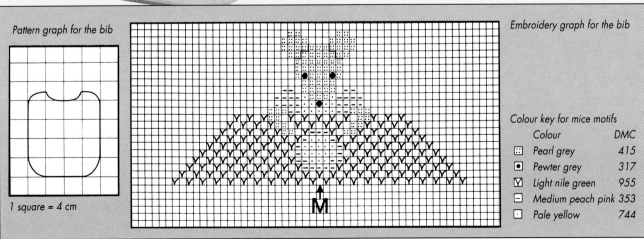

Pattern graph for the bib

1 square = 4 cm

Embroidery graph for the bib

M

Colour key for mice motifs

	Colour	DMC
⊡	Pearl grey	415
⊙	Pewter grey	317
Y	Light nile green	955
–	Medium peach pink	353
⬚	Pale yellow	744

COVERALL

Materials

60 cm of 90 cm wide pink and white striped cotton
18 x 22 cm piece of 11 count white Aida fabric
DMC stranded embroidery cottons in the colours indicated on the colour key
Bias binding: 90 cm pale green, 85 cm pale yellow, 75 cm white.

Finished size Embroidery 5 x 8.5 cm. See the General Instructions and Stitch Library on pages 92–6.

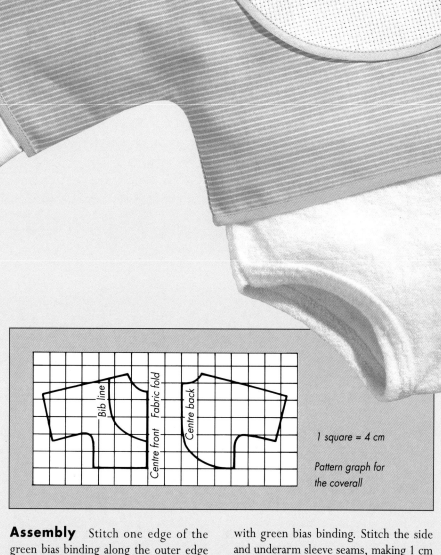

1 square = 4 cm

Pattern graph for the coverall

Method Enlarge the pattern graph and cut out the paper pattern. Copy the bib section of the front on the indicated line. Open the bib piece to obtain a full pattern. Outline the bib on the Aida fabric with running stitches. Following the graph, embroider the two mice in cross stitch. Start the embroidery with the right foot, 12 fabric squares away from the centre, and 4.5 cm up from the lower edge of the bib. Work each cross over one fabric square, using two strands of embroidery cotton. When the cross stitching is complete, work the outlines in backstitch, using pewter grey number 317. When the embroidery is complete, cut the bib pattern on the marked outline, adding a 1 cm wide seam allowance at the shoulders.

Adding a 1 cm wide seam allowance, cut the front once on the fabric fold and the back twice from striped fabric: place the patterns along the stripes of the fabric, and cut the edges that are finished with bias binding without a seam allowance.

Assembly Stitch one edge of the green bias binding along the outer edge onto the wrong side of the bib. Fold the bias binding around the seam, place the bib on the front, and stitch in position. Stitch the shoulder seams, making 1 cm wide seams. Finish the lower sleeve edges with green bias binding. Stitch the side and underarm sleeve seams, making 1 cm wide seams. Finish the lower edge and the centre back edges of the coverall with yellow bias binding. Finish the neck edge with white bias binding, extending it about 25 cm to form ties.

SHEET

Materials

1.25 m of 100 cm wide green, white and apricot striped cotton
8.5 cm x 1.10 m piece of 11 count white Aida
DMC stranded embroidery cottons in the colours indicated on the colour key

Finished size   Sheet measures about 100 x 125 cm. Embroidered border is about 6.5 cm wide.
See the General Instructions and Stitch Library on pages 92–6.

Method   Following the graph, embroider the motif of two mice in the centre of the fabric strip. Work each cross stitch over one fabric square, using two strands of embroidery cotton. When the cross stitching is complete, work the outlines in backstitch, using pewter grey number 317. Repeat the design for the required length.

To finish   Make a narrow hem along the sides and lower edge of the sheet. Baste a 5.5 cm wide hem, with 1 cm turned under, along the top edge. Stitch the embroidered band, with the raw edges turned under (1 cm seam allowance included on top and bottom edges), onto the sheet. Position the lower edge of the band 5.25 cm from the top edge of the sheet.

or a festive outdoor meal, lay a garden table with this pretty cloth, covered with its exuberant design of apples and apple blossom. The cloth is square (about 135 x 135 cm), and the embroidered wreath is round. The matching serviettes are decorated with an apple motif from the cloth.

TABLE

TABLECLOTH

Materials

1.50 m of 150 cm wide hardanger fabric with 9 double fabric threads to 1 cm
DMC stranded embroidery cottons in the colours indicated on the colour key on foldout sheet F

Finished size Tablecloth about 135 cm square.
Embroidered wreath is about 45 cm in diameter.
The graph is on foldout sheet F.
See the General Instructions and Stitch Library on pages 92–6.

Method Mark the centre of the cloth with one vertical and one horizontal line in running stitch. Following the graph, embroider the motif in cross stitch. Work each cross over two double fabric threads using three strands of embroidery cotton. When the cross stitching is complete, work the outlines in backstitch using two strands of cotton.

Start the embroidery at A, 204 double fabric threads from the centre. Repeat the motif three more times to complete the design. When the embroidery is complete, work a row of crosses in dark forest green number 987 around the cloth, 9 cm inside the edges. Leave a space of two double fabric threads between each cross.

To finish Baste a 3 cm wide double hem around the cloth. Make mitred corners. Secure the hem against the back of the row of crosses.

SERVIETTES

Materials

For one serviette
42 cm square piece of hardanger fabric with 9 double fabric threads to 1 cm
DMC stranded embroidery cottons in the colours indicated on the colour key

Finished size 36 cm square.

See the General Instructions and Stitch Library on pages 92–6.

Method Using dark forest green number 987, embroider a 33 cm square in the centre of the fabric. Work in cross stitch over two double fabric threads, using three strands of embroidery cotton. Leave two double fabric threads between each cross. Following the graph, embroider the apple motif in one corner.

To finish Baste a 1.5 cm wide double hem along the serviette edges. Make mitred corners. Secure the hem against the back of the row of crosses.

Cross stitch graph for the serviette

Colour key for the serviette

Colour		DMC
⊡	Very light topaz	727
⊟	Lemon	307
⊞	Topaz	725
☑	Christmas gold	783
◹	Light pumpkin	970
☒	Dark coral	349
⊠	Medium bright red	304
⊡	White	White
⊟	Light avocado green	470
⊠	Dark forest green	987
⊡	Light brown	434
■	Dark coffee brown	801

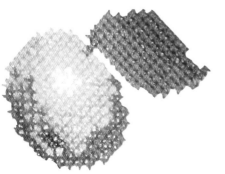

WILDFLOWER SAMPLER

*S*eventeen different wild plants of Europe are illustrated on this magnificent sampler. Some, such as rose hips, dandelion and ivy, will be easily recognised. Others, such as flax, wild chicory and snub pea, are perhaps less well known, but together they make a beautiful picture that will be a delight to stitch.

PICTURE

Materials

65 x 80 cm piece of ecru linen 10 or 11
DMC stranded embroidery cottons in the colours indicated on the colour key on foldout sheet D
Optional: a matching frame

Finished Size Framed picture 45.5 x 60 cm, embroidery about 40 x 54 cm. The graph is on foldout sheet D.
See the General Instructions and Stitch Library on pages 92–6.

Method Following the graph, embroider the motifs in cross stitch. Work the crosses over two fabric threads, using two strands of embroidery cotton. When cross stitching is complete, work the outlines and details in backstitch, using one strand of cotton (or two strands when indicated on the graph). Start the embroidery at A in the right lower corner, 14 cm from the edges.

To finish Frame the completed embroidery, or finish it as preferred.

DUCKS IN THE BATH

Embroider a happy duck on a toilet bag made from bright yellow Aida fabric. The bag is lined and is closed with a zipper. And to match, you could decorate a towel with an Aida band embroidered with a row of cheerful ducks. These two simple projects in bright colours would make a perfect gift.

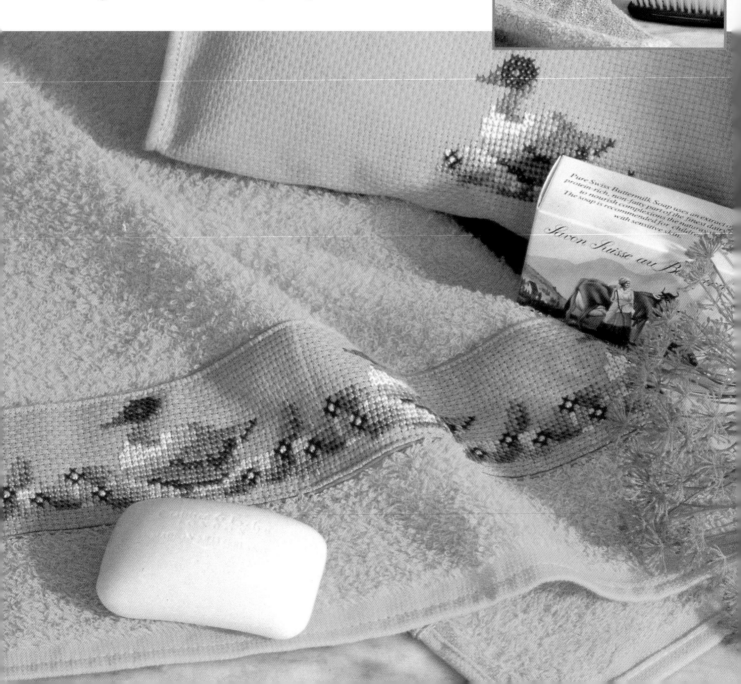

TOILET BAG

Materials

Orange-yellow 11 count Aida fabric, one piece 25 x 35 cm, and two gusset strips 5 x 13 cm (if this rich colour is not available, dye white Aida)
Lining White cotton fabric in pieces the same size as Aida
A 24 cm long zipper
1.50 m blue bias binding
DMC stranded embroidery cottons in the colours indicated on the colour key

Finished size Bag 15 x 25 cm. Embroidery 5 x 7.5 cm.
See the General Instructions and Stitch Library on pages 92–6.

Method Following the graph, embroider the motif in cross stitch. Work each cross over one fabric square, using three strands of embroidery cotton. Start the embroidery at A, 4 cm from the right edge (one long side) and 13 cm from the top edge (one short side).

Assembly Place the Aida pieces and lining pieces together with *wrong sides* facing, and baste them together along the edges. Finish the short edges (top edges) of the bag, as well as one short side of the gussets, with bias binding. Stitch the zipper between the finished top edges of the bag. Place the lower edge of the gussets onto the bag, with the lined sides facing, and with the centre of the gusset matching the centre of one long side. Sew the lower edge, and then the side edges of the gussets between the bag, making a 5 mm wide seam. Cut the seam corners diagonally. Finish the sides of the bag all around with bias binding. Sew a 10 cm long piece of bias binding in half across its width. Knot this around the zipper tag and make a knot in the ends.

TOWEL BORDER

Materials

A yellow bath towel
10 cm wide orange-yellow 11 count Aida fabric, as long as the width of the towel plus about 5 cm for turnings (if this rich colour is not available, dye white Aida)
Light blue bias binding
DMC stranded embroidery cottons in the colours indicated on the colour key

Finished size Width of border about 6.5 cm.
See the General Instructions and Stitch Library on pages 92–6.

Method Following the graph, embroider the motif in cross stitch. Work each cross over one fabric square, using three strands of embroidery cotton. Start the embroidery 2 cm from the lower edge (one long side). Repeat the design for the desired length.

To finish Press the folds out of the bias binding, and press it in half across its width. Fold the top and bottom edges of the embroidered piece to the back, two fabric squares away from the embroidery. Baste a piece of bias binding along both the top and bottom edges, against the back of the Aida fabric, leaving a narrow edge of the bias binding visible at the front. Turn the short ends to the wrong side, and stitch the band in position.

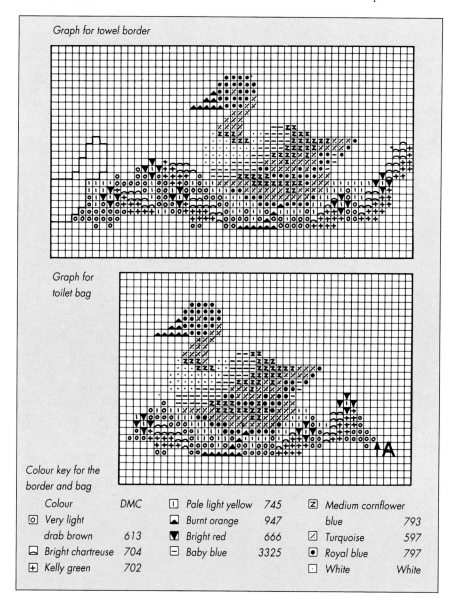

Graph for towel border

Graph for toilet bag

Colour key for the border and bag

	Colour	DMC
⊙	Very light drab brown	613
☐	Bright chartreuse	704
✦	Kelly green	702

		DMC
⊡	Pale light yellow	745
▲	Burnt orange	947
▼	Bright red	666
⊟	Baby blue	3325

		DMC
☑	Medium cornflower blue	793
⊠	Turquoise	597
⊙	Royal blue	797
☐	White	White

FOR THE FESTIVE SEASON

SUITABLE FOR BEGINNERS

*H*ere's an embroidery idea for the festive season: cross stitch cards decorated with a Christmas tree, bell or tree ornaments. They make a greeting very special, and will delight friends and family, but they are quite simple to make.

CARDS

See the General Instructions and Stitch Library on pages 92–6.

Materials

Small pieces of different coloured evenweave fabric with 10 fabric threads to 1 cm
Small amounts of stranded embroidery cottons
Strong paper in various colours, or purchased card mounts

Method Following the selected graphs, embroider the motifs in the centre of the fabric pieces. Work in cross stitch over two fabric threads using two strands of embroidery cotton. When the cross stitching is complete, work the outlines in backstitch using two strands of cotton. Fold the paper into cards and glue the embroideries on the front. Or cut away a window in the front and glue the embroideries behind the window, and glue a piece of paper over the back of the embroidery.

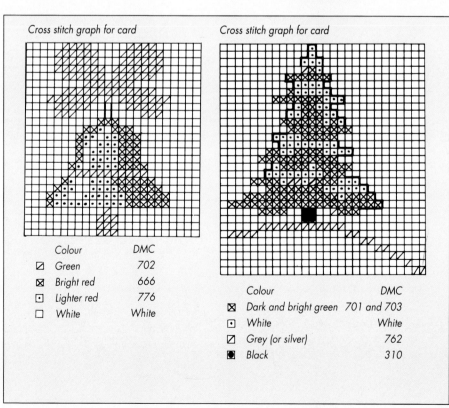

Cross stitch graph for card

Colour	DMC
☑ Green	702
☒ Bright red	666
⊡ Lighter red	776
☐ White	White

Cross stitch graph for card

Colour	DMC
☒ Dark and bright green	701 and 703
⊡ White	White
⧄ Grey (or silver)	762
⬛ Black	310

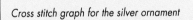

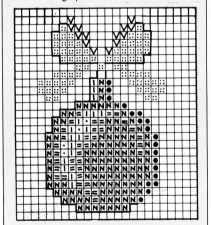

Cross stitch graphs for the red and white ornaments

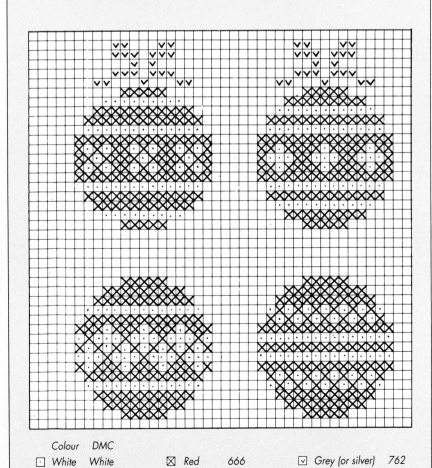

Colour	DMC				
White	White	⊠ Red	666	☑ Grey (or silver)	762

Cross stitch graph for the silver ornament

Colour	DMC		
⊡ White	White	Ⓘ Very light grey	762
⊞ Light green	703	⊟ Light grey	415
☑ Green	701	Ⓝ Grey	318
		● Dark Grey	414

Outlines Use dark grey around the ball, and green around the bow.

A TRADITIONAL SAMPLER

*H*ere is an authentic nineteenth century sampler for you to copy that is more than 150 years old. And there are plenty of ideas for ways of using the motifs from the sampler, if you prefer a simpler project. Make a needlecase, a runner, shelf border, handkerchief or book cover. We include instructions for all of these, but the possibilities are endless.

Materials

70 cm square piece of linen 14
DMC stranded embroidery cottons
in the colours indicated on the
colour key on foldout sheet B
Optional: a frame

Note The linen for this project is very fine, so you may prefer to choose a coarser one. When selecting linen with fewer fabric threads to 1 cm, use a larger piece, because the motifs will turn out larger. Also, choose embroidery cottons in one tone lighter; you will also need more thread.

Finished size About 50 x 52 cm. The graph is on foldout sheets B and C. See the General Instructions and Stitch Library on pages 92–6.

Method Following the graph, work the sampler motifs on the linen. Work in cross stitch over two fabric threads, using one strand of embroidery cotton. Start the embroidery with the border at the lower right corner, about 10 cm from the edges.

Work the snake of the Adam and Eve motif in backstitch or chain stitch, using number 420. Embroider the crowns at top left and in the centre in star stitch, using numbers 420 and 422. Following the alphabet and number graphs, embroider your initials and the year of work in the spaces used by the original embroiderer.

To finish Finish the sampler with an openwork hem, or frame it as desired.

Alphabet and number graphs for the sampler

SHELF BORDERS

Materials

White linen band, about 6 cm wide, with 10 fabric threads to 1 cm in the desired length, or an 8 cm wide strip of linen in the desired length
DMC stranded embroidery cottons in the colours indicated on the colour key on foldout sheet B

Finished size Border is about 6 cm wide.
The graph is on foldout sheets B and C. See the General Instructions and Stitch Library on pages 92–6.

Method Following the graph for the sampler, work the basket or deer motif in cross stitch, leaving a space of twenty fabric threads between each motif. Work the crosses over two fabric threads, using two strands of embroidery cotton. Repeat the motif for the required length. Using number 367, work a few cross stitches between the baskets, and work a row of cross stitches below the deer motifs; if necessary, refer to the photographs of the finished borders. Finish the short sides of the band with a narrow hem. If using a strip of linen, finish the long edges too (1 cm hem allowance added at top and bottom).

NEEDLECASE

Materials

14 x 15 cm piece of ecru linen 12
DMC stranded embroidery cottons
in the colours indicated on the
colour key on foldout sheet B, plus
sky blue number 519
Lining 12 x 13 cm piece of fabric
About 7 x 12 cm piece of light
blue felt
11 x 12 cm piece of fusible
interfacing

Finished size About 6 x 11 cm.
The graph is on foldout sheet B.

See the General Instructions and Stitch
Library on pages 92–6.

Method Following the graph of the
sampler, embroider the motif in cross
stitch over two fabric threads, using one
strand of embroidery cotton. Work the
centre of the motif 3.75 cm from the
lower edge (one long side) and 4.5 cm
from the right side edge. When all cross
stitching is complete, work the details in
backstitch, using number 420.

To finish Iron the interfacing to the
wrong side of the linen in the centre of
the embroidery. Fold the seams to the
wrong side around the edges of the
interfacing. Secure the seams to the
interfacing with herringbone stitch,
forming mitred corners.

Using stranded embroidery cotton
number 519, twist a cord about 90 cm
long. From this cut a 26 cm long piece and
sew it along the top edge and halfway
down the side edges of the needlecase.
Repeat with remaining cord, and glue this
along lower edge and halfway up the side
edges, but extend the ends about 19 cm
for ties for closing the case.

Turn under the 1 cm seam allowance
of the lining. Place it on the embroidered
piece with wrong sides facing and sew it
in place. Make a vertical row of back-
stitching along centre of book, working
through all layers. Using pinking shears,
cut the felt into a piece 5.5 x 10.5 cm and
glue it to the inside of needlecase.

SUITABLE FOR BEGINNERS

RUNNER

Materials

20.5 x 94 cm ecru linen 14
DMC stranded embroidery cottons
in the colours indicated on the
colour key on foldout sheet B
40 cm of lace, about 1.5 cm wide

Finished size 16.5 x 90 cm. The
embroidered area measures 11.5 x
5.5 cm.
See the General Instructions and Stitch
Library on pages 92–6.

Method Turn a 1 cm wide double
hem to the *right side* of the cloth and
baste in place. Cut and withdraw two
fabric threads above the hem to the
corner. Darn the short ends of the cut
fabric threads back into the fabric at
the corners, and finish the seam with
straight corners. Secure the hem with

Cross stitch graph for the runner

DMC	Colour
⊡ Dark navy blue	823
⊠ Dark yellow-green	3345
⧄ Very light olive-green	834
⊡ Light hazelnut brown	422
⊟ Dark hazelnut brown	420

open hemstitch worked over four
fabric threads.

Following the graph of the
peacocks, embroider the motif along
the short sides of the cloth. Work in
cross stitch over two fabric threads,

using one strand of embroidery cotton.
Position M in the centre of the cloth,
4.5 cm from the short edges. Sew the
lace below the motif onto the hem, and
finish the short ends of the lace with a
narrow rolled seam.

BOOKCOVER

Materials

A book
A piece of light blue linen 12
measuring the height of the book
plus 2 cm, and the same width as
the front, spine, and back of the
book plus 13 cm
DMC stranded embroidery cottons
in the colours indicated on the
colour key for the sampler (on
foldout sheet B), plus light
Wedgwood blue, number 518
Lining
A piece of fabric the same size as
the linen

Finished size The embroidered area
is 9 cm square.
The graph is on foldout sheet C.
See the General Instructions and Stitch
Library on pages 92–6.

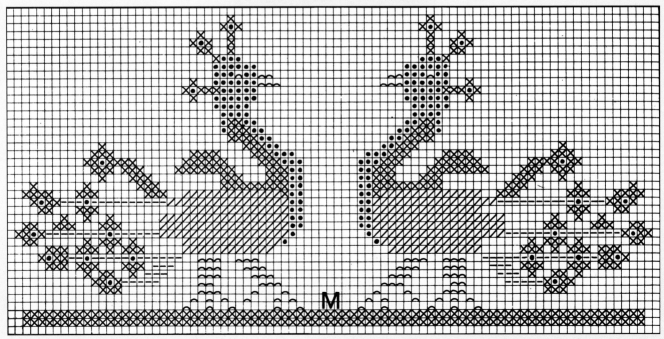

Method Place the linen around the book, overlapping the top and bottom edges 1 cm, and the side edges 6.5 cm. Decide on the placement of the motif on the front of the cover. Following the graph of the sampler, embroider the church motif in cross stitch over two fabric threads, using one strand of embroidery cotton. When complete, embroider a row of cross stitches along the top and bottom edges, using two strands number 518; position the rows about 1.5 cm from the edges and leave a space of two fabric threads between each cross.

HANDKERCHIEF

Materials

A white handkerchief
DMC stranded embroidery cottons in the colours indicated on the colour key on foldout sheet B
6 x 8 cm piece waste canvas with 12 fabric threads to 1 cm

Finished size The embroidery is about 3 x 4 cm.

The graph is on fold-out sheet B.

See the General Instructions and Stitch Library on pages 92–6.

Method Baste the waste canvas diagonally over a corner of the handkerchief. Following the graph of the sampler, embroider the basket motif in cross stitch over the centre of the waste canvas; position the lower edge of the motif 3 cm from the corner. Work the crosses over two fabric threads, using two strands of embroidery cotton. Keep the needle perpendicular to the canvas while working, and stitch only through the canvas holes, not the canvas threads. When complete, remove the basting and carefully pull out the canvas threads one by one with tweezers.

To finish With right sides facing, stitch the embroidered piece and the lining together, making a 1 cm wide seam, and leaving a small opening on one of the side seams for turning through. Cut corners diagonally, turn through, and slipstitch the opening closed. Fold both short sides 5.5 cm towards the middle and hand sew in place along the top and bottom edges. Slip the book inside the cover.

SUITABLE FOR BEGINNERS

LITTLE FLOWER PICTURES

*H*ere are three delicate little flower embroideries in cross stitch! Their special hangers, a piece of ribbon, give a pretty finish.

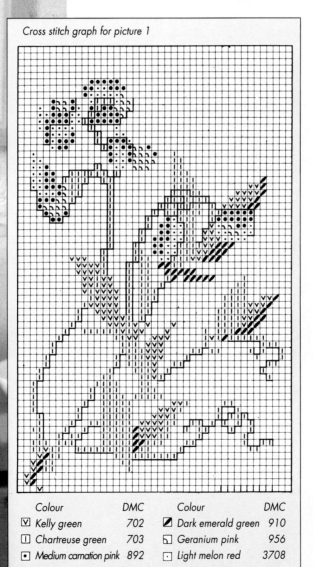

Cross stitch graph for picture 1

Colour	DMC		Colour	DMC
☑ Kelly green	702		☒ Dark emerald green	910
⊡ Chartreuse green	703		☒ Geranium pink	956
⊙ Medium carnation pink	892		⊡ Light melon red	3708

Outlines In and around the flowers with bright red 666; along the stems and leaves in dark emerald green 910.

FLOWER PICTURES

Materials

For each picture
35 cm square piece of white linen 11
DMC stranded embroidery cottons in the colours indicated on the colour key, and also for picture 1: bright red 666; for picture 2: very dark royal blue 820
A matching frame

Finished size About 19 cm square, when framed.
See the General Instructions and Stitch Library on pages 92–6.

Method Following the graph, embroider the motif in the centre of the linen. Work in cross stitch over two fabric threads using two strands of embroidery cotton. When the cross stitching is complete, work the outlines in backstitch using two strands of cotton.

To finish Frame when completed.

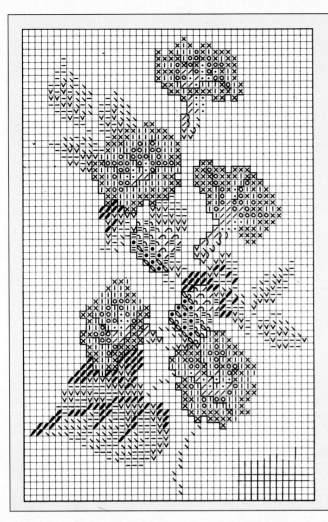

Cross stitch graph for picture 2

Colour key for picture 2

	Colour	DMC
⊡	Medium bright red	304
◨	Deep rose	309
⊟	Rose	335
☑	Pearl grey	415
▨	Kelly green	702
⊟	Chartreuse green	703
◪	Very light pine green	772
⊡	Light baby blue	775
⊠	Royal blue	797
◫	Medium Delft blue	799
⊙	Pale Delft blue	800
◱	Medium rose	899
◪	Dark emerald green	910
◳	Baby green	966
◩	Light rose	3326

Outlines In and around the blue flowers in very dark royal blue 820; around the pink flowers in medium bright red 304; and along the flower stems in dark emerald green 910.

Cross stitch graph for picture 3

Colour key for picture 3

	Colour	DMC
◨	White	White
☑	Very dark lavender	208
◪	Dark lavender	209
◨	Dark blue-violet	333
⊟	Kelly green	702
⊡	Chartreuse green	703
⊟	Medium tangerine	741
◼	Very dark cornflower blue	791
⊠	Dark emerald green	910
◫	Baby green	966

Outlines In and around the flowers in very dark cornflower blue 791; in and along the leaves in dark emerald green 910.

FRESH FRUITS AND BERRIES

SUITABLE FOR BEGINNERS

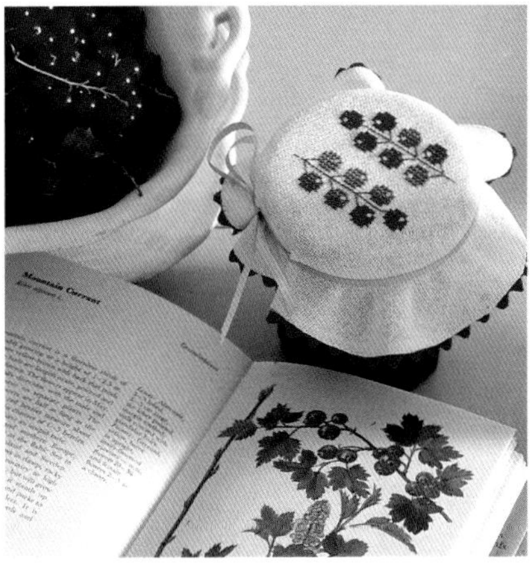

Looking for a personal gift? Embroidered jam lid covers are quick and easy to make and add a special touch to a gift of jams or preserves. They can be finished in different ways, as the photograph illustrates.

JAM LID COVER

Materials

For one cover
20 cm square piece of white linen 10 or 11
DMC stranded embroidery cottons in the colours indicated on the colour key.
Optional 55 cm red ricrac band

Finished size About 16 cm in diameter, 17 cm square and 20 cm square. See the General Instructions and Stitch Library on pages 92–6.

Method Following the graph, embroider the selected motif in the centre of the fabric. Work each cross stitch over two fabric threads, using two strands embroidery cotton. When all cross stitching is complete, work the details in backstitch, using Kelly green number 702.

To finish For the round cover, cut the fabric into a 17 cm diameter circle. Sew the raw edge under 5 mm, adding the ricrac band at the same time on the back. For the small square cover, cut the fabric into an 18 cm square, and sew the raw edge under 5 mm all around. For the large square, stitch a line of zigzag stitches all around, about 7.5 mm from the edges. Withdraw the fabric threads up to the stitchline to form fringes.

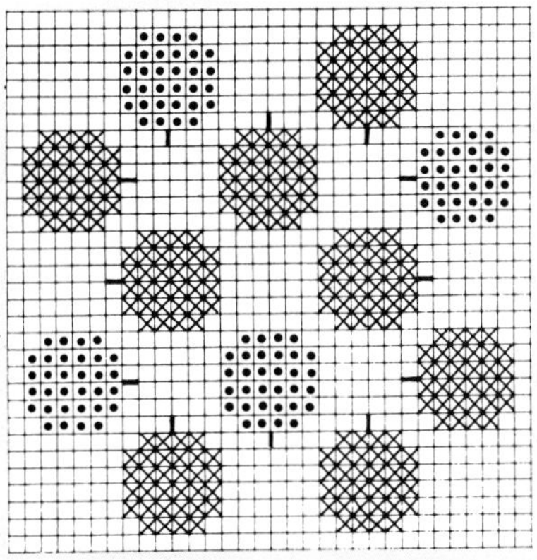

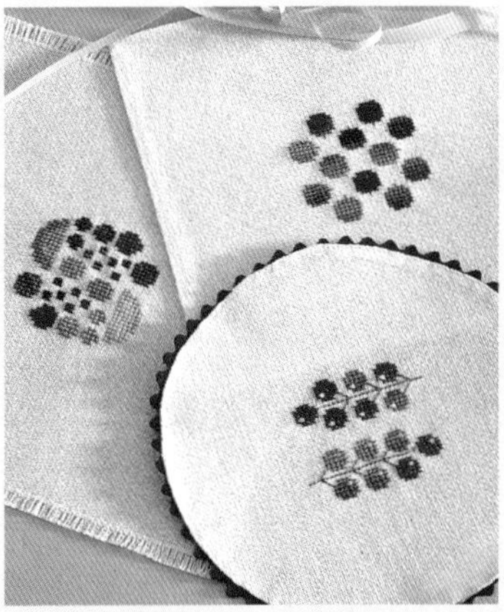

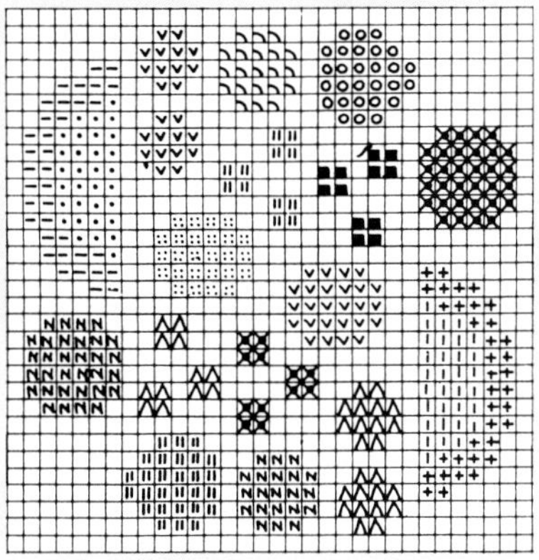

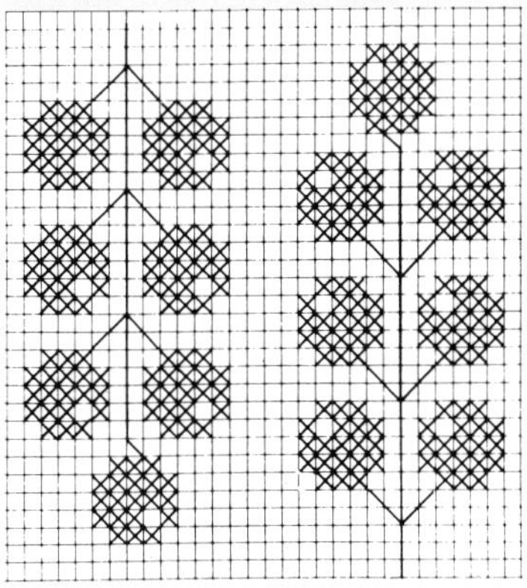

Colour key for the jam lid covers

Colour	DMC	Colour	DMC	Colour	DMC
☒ *Red variegated*	57	⊡ *Coral*	351	◫ *Medium tangerine*	741
◙ *Mauve variegated*	102	Ⓝ *Very dark cranberry*	600	⊡ *Lemon*	307
◎ *Bright red*	666	⊠ *Dark violet*	552	⊟ *Light canary yellow*	973
◺ *Very dark coral*	817	◫ *Bright red orange*	606	☑ *Light green*	471
◼ *Very dark garnet*	902	◹ *Light pumpkin*	970	**Backstitching:** *Kelly green number 702*	
		⊞ *Burnt orange*	947		

Y ou will find them in the forest…mushrooms…at
times hidden beneath a blanket of fallen leaves. This
exquisite picture with eleven mushrooms will be a real
winner for all nature lovers. It is not necessary to embroider
all the mushrooms of the picture: they are also beautiful on their own.
Embroider one on a pincushion, and frame it with a matching border.

PICTURE

Materials

One 65 cm square piece of white linen 10 or 11
DMC stranded embroidery cottons in the colours indicated on the colour key on foldout sheet F
A matching frame

Finished size Framed picture about 44 cm square.

The cross stitch graph is on foldout sheet F.

See the General Instructions and Stitch Library on pages 92–6.

Method Following the graph, embroider the motif on the linen. Work in cross stitch over two fabric threads using two strands of embroidery cotton. Start the embroidery in the right lower corner with the outer frame, 13 cm inside the edges. When the cross stitching is complete, work the outlines in backstitch using one strand of embroidery cotton, except for the grass blades, which should be worked with two strands.

To finish Frame the completed embroidery or finish it as preferred.

PINCUSHION

Materials

12 x 24 cm piece of white linen 10 or 11
DMC stranded embroidery cottons in the colours indicated on the colour key for the picture
Synthetic fibrefill or wool scraps

Finished size About 10 cm square.

The graph is on foldout sheet F.

See the General Instructions and Stitch Library on pages 92–6.

Method Cut the fabric into two 12 cm square pieces. Following the graph for the picture, embroider the small red mushrooms in the centre of one piece. Work in cross stitch over two fabric threads using two strands of embroidery cotton. Omit the grass blades and the green crosses on the left. When the cross stitching is complete, work the outlines in backstitch using one strand of cotton. Using bright red, work an 8.5 cm square frame of crosses around the design. Leave two fabric threads between each cross.

To finish Making 1 cm wide seams, sew the two linen pieces together with right sides facing, leaving a small opening for turning. Cut the seam corners diagonally, turn the pincushion through and fill with fibrefill or scraps of wool left over from knitting or embroidery. Slipstitch the opening closed.

SWEET
VIOLETS

A tablecloth with a teacosy to match makes a very enjoyable project. The tablecloth has a band of sweet violets in the centre, and single flowers strewn at random over the cloth. The teacosy also has violets sprinkled over its surface and, like the tablecloth, is finished with bias binding.

TABLECLOTH

Materials

1.95 m of 150 cm wide pale grey hardanger with 9 double fabric threads to 1 cm
Anchor stranded embroidery cottons in the colours in colour key (foldout sheet E), and black number 0403
7 m matching blue bias binding

Finished size About 194 x 146 cm. The embroidered band is about 27 cm wide.

The graph is on foldout sheet E.

See the General Instructions and Stitch Library on pages 92–6.

Method Cut the fabric into a piece measuring 194 x 146 cm. Finish the edges with bias binding. Following the graph, embroider the motif in cross stitch. Work the crosses over two double fabric threads, using three strands of embroidery thread. When all the cross stitching is complete, work the outlines in backstitch, using two strands of thread. Start the embroidery at A, in the centre of the right side (one short side), 3.5 cm from the blue bias binding. Repeat the motif 5.5 times, until the band reaches a point 3.5 cm from the short left side. When completed, work single violets strewn over the cloth. Position motifs as preferred; use pieces of paper as a guide to work out placement on the cloth.

TEACOSY

Materials

45 cm of 150 cm wide pale grey hardanger with 9 double fabric threads to 1 cm

1.00 m of 90 cm wide cotton for the inner cosy

Anchor stranded embroidery cottons in the colours indicated on the colour key (foldout sheet E), and black number 0403

1 m bias binding in two matching blues

Synthetic fibrefill

Finished size About 36 x 28 cm. The graph is on foldout sheet E. See the General Instructions and Stitch Library on pages 92–6.

Method From the hardanger fabric cut two pieces about 45 x 39 cm, and for the gusset one strip about 95 x 6 cm.

Enlarge the pattern graph for the cosy and cut out the paper pattern. Using running stitches, mark the outline of the pattern on each piece of hardanger, 6 cm from the lower edge.

Following the graph for the tablecloth, embroider single violets in cross stitch over the two pieces. Work the crosses over two double fabric threads, using three strands of embroidery cotton. Position the motifs as preferred, using small pieces of paper to work out their placement on the fabric. When completed, cut the embroidered pieces, adding 5 mm seam and 6 cm wide hem allowances.

Assembly In assembling the outer and inner cosies, sew all pieces together with *wrong sides* facing, making 5 mm wide seams. Sew the gusset between the front and back piece. Finish the seams with two colours of bias binding.

Inner cosy The inner cosy is made of two cosies with filling between. From cotton, cut four cosy shapes, adding a 1 cm wide seam allowance, and two gusset strips about 83 x 7 cm. Sew a gusset between two cosy shapes. Repeat for the remaining pieces. Turn one cosy right side out. Put the inner cosies together with wrong sides facing and put the fibre filling between. Close the lower edge with the seams turned inwards. Put the inside cosy into the cover. Fold the hem of the cover to the wrong side, and secure it by hand against the inner cosy with a small turning.

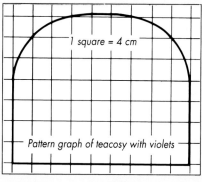

1 square = 4 cm

Pattern graph of teacosy with violets

SMILING DWARFS

The happy dwarf atop his ladder decorating this bright placemat will bring a smile at every meal. And there's a special serviette ring to match. Little boys and girls will also like this laundry or pyjama bag, which completes the group — and even beginner embroiderers will find it quick and easy to make.

PLACEMAT

Materials

48 x 34 cm piece of white
11 count Aida fabric
Small quantities of bias binding in pink, yellow, turquoise and red DMC stranded embroidery cottons in the colours in the colour key

Finished size 48 x 34 cm.
See the General Instructions and Stitch Library on pages 92–6.

Method Following the graph, embroider the motif in cross stitch. Work the crosses over one fabric square, using three strands of embroidery cotton. Start the embroidery with the right lower stitch of the ladder, 8 cm from the short side at the left, and 2 cm from the long side (lower edge). When all cross stitching is complete, work the outlines in backstitch, using two strands of embroidery cotton.

To finish Finish the placemat all around with bias binding, using a different colour for each side.

Graph for laundry bag and serviette ring

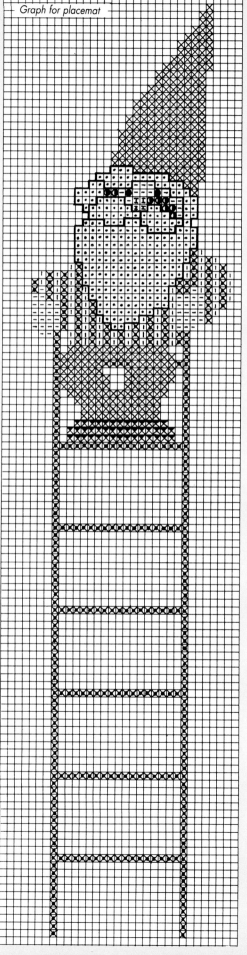

Graph for placemat

SERVIETTE RING

Materials

Two 5.5 x 17 cm pieces of 11 count white Aida
35 cm turquoise bias binding
A button
DMC stranded embroidery cottons for the bucket motif, in the colours indicated on the colour key for the placemat

Finished size 5.5 x 15 cm.
See the General Instructions and Stitch Library on pages 92–6.

Method Following the graph, embroider the motif in cross stitch. Start at A with the bottom row of the motif. Position it about 1 cm up from the lower edge (one long side),

Colour key for Smiling dwarfs laundry bag and placemat

	Colour	DMC
☒	Bright red	666
☒	Medium Wedgwood blue	517
·	White	White
⊡	Light rose	3326
⊟	Very light flesh	951
◐	Pale pink	353
⊞	Pearl grey	415
◨	Dark steel grey	414
⊡	Medium electric blue	996
⊔	Deep canary yellow	973
☒	Dark cornflower blue	792
⊙	Black	310

Outlines *The hair and beard of dwarf in dark steel grey 414, trousers in dark cornflower blue 792; berries in black.*

matching A with the centre of the fabric. Work the crosses over one fabric square, using three strands of embroidery cotton. When all cross stitching is complete, work the outlines in backstitch, using two strands of cotton. Using black cotton, twist a cord for the handle of the bucket, and secure the ends onto the bucket.

To finish Place the two pieces of Aida fabric together with *wrong sides* together. Fold the short ends of each piece to the wrong side and secure with small stitches. Finish the long sides with bias binding; position it two fabric squares away from the embroidery at the top edge, and one fabric square away at the bottom edge. Make a buttonhole loop on one end and sew the button on the other end to close the serviette ring.

LAUNDRY BAG

Materials

Two 46 x 60 cm pieces of white Hertarette fabric (DMC article number 3611) with 3 fabric squares to 1 cm
90 cm of wide turquoise bias binding
10 transparent plastic rings
1.35 m cotton cord
DMC stranded embroidery cottons in the colours in the colour key

Finished size 44 x 58 cm
See the General Instructions and Stitch Library on pages 92–6.

Method Following the graph, embroider the motif in the centre of one piece of Hertarette, 6 cm from one short side (bottom edge of bag). Work in cross stitch over two fabric squares, using six strands of embroidery cotton. When all cross stitching is complete, work the details in backstitch, using three strands of cotton. For the handle of the bucket, couch the ends of a short length of thread onto the bucket.

To finish With right sides together, and making a 1 cm wide seam, sew the two pieces of Hertarette together along the sides and lower edge. Cut the seam corners diagonally and finish the seams thoroughly. Turn the bag right side out. Finish the top edge with bias binding. Sew the plastic rings to the bag; position them 7 cm from the top edge and leave about 9 cm between each ring. Lace the cord through the rings to close the bag.

COOL BLUES

*S*imple stitching and just two blues make this an easy but elegant project. The little birds are traditional sampler motifs, given a modern look in this design.

SMALL MAT

Materials

40 cm square piece of ecru linen 10 or 11
DMC stranded embroidery cottons, dark Delft blue 798 and Delft blue 809

Finished size 28 cm square.
See the General Instructions and Stitch Library on pages 92–6.

Method Following the graph, embroider the motif on the linen. Work each cross stitch over two fabric threads using two strands of embroidery cotton. Start the embroidery at M, in the centre and 8.5 cm from the edges. To complete the motif, repeat it three more times.

To finish Cut the embroidered piece into a 34 cm square. Baste a 1.5 cm double hem all around the cloth. Above the hem remove two fabric threads up to the corners where these threads intersect; darn the small ends of the threads back into the fabric. Make mitred corners in the hem. Secure the hem with open hemstitch worked over two fabric threads, with one strand of number 809 embroidery cotton.

Colour key for the cloth		
Colour		DMC
⊡ Dark delft blue		798
⊙ Delft blue		809

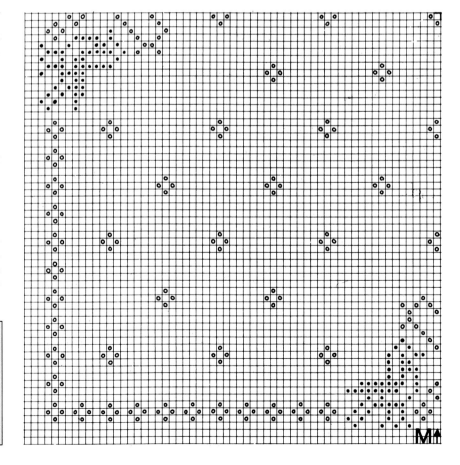

COLOURFUL PICNICS

A day out in the country is not complete without a picnic. Make the occasion extra special with this red picnic cloth and matching basket to hold all kinds of gourmet delights. The fresh summer bouquets and geometric designs combine well with the warm red background fabric.

PICNIC CLOTH

Materials

1.35 m of 140 cm wide red 11 count Aida fabric
Lining 1.30 m of 140 cm wide red cotton fabric
Anchor stranded embroidery cottons in the colours indicated on the colour key
A 150 cm square piece of batting or pre-washed flannel

Finished size 128 cm square.
See the General Instructions and Stitch Library on pages 92–6.

Method Read the complete instructions first before starting. Following the graph, embroider the horizontal and vertical borders in cross stitch. Work each cross over one fabric square using two strands of embroidery cotton. Start the embroidery in the

right lower corner, 6 cm from the side edge and 23.5 cm from the lower edge. Embroider the horizontal borders first, then the vertical borders. The inside area of the resulting blocks is 21 cm square. Following the layout, interrupt the borders on the indicated spots for the flower bouquets: the arrows indicate the direction of the bouquets. When the cross stitching is complete, work the outlines in backstitch, using two strands of embroidery cotton. Following the graph, embroider the small block motifs to form triangles, using alternating colours for each small block. Position them in the corners as indicated on the layout, three fabric squares from the embroidered border.

To finish Cut the embroidered piece and the lining into 130 cm squares. Place them together with right sides facing, and the batting on top. Pin and sew together, making 1 cm wide seams, and leaving an opening on one side for turning. Cut the seam corners diagonally, pull through, and slipstitch the opening closed. Quilt through all

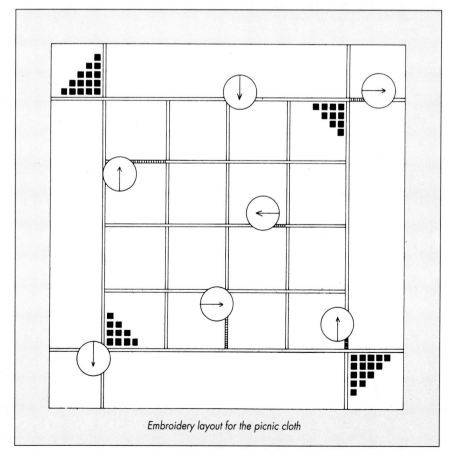

Embroidery layout for the picnic cloth

Embroidery graph for the flower bouquet

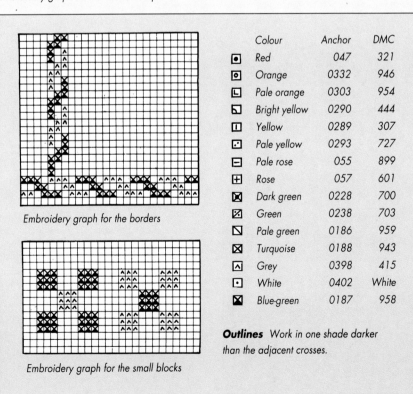

Embroidery graph for the borders

Embroidery graph for the small blocks

	Colour	Anchor	DMC
⊙	Red	047	321
◉	Orange	0332	946
⊡	Pale orange	0303	954
◪	Bright yellow	0290	444
⊞	Yellow	0289	307
⊡	Pale yellow	0293	727
⊟	Pale rose	055	899
⊞	Rose	057	601
⊠	Dark green	0228	700
⧄	Green	0238	703
◹	Pale green	0186	959
⊠	Turquoise	0188	943
◹	Grey	0398	415
⊡	White	0402	White
⊠	Blue-green	0187	958

Outlines Work in one shade darker than the adjacent crosses.

three layers along the four outer horizontal and vertical embroidered borders, using a small running stitch.

PICNIC BASKET

Materials

40 x 60 cm piece of red 11 count Aida fabric
Anchor stranded embroidery cottons in the colours indicated on the colour key
Elastic

Finished size Basket about 38 x 49 cm.
See the General Instructions and Stitch Library on pages 92–6.

Note For a different-sized basket, measure its length and width. Then cut the two fabric pieces with 1 cm extra at the sides and lower edge, and 4.5 cm extra at the top edge for the casing.

Method Cut the Aida fabric in two 30 x 40 cm pieces. Following the graph for the picnic cloth, embroider the bouquet on both fabric pieces. Work each cross stitch over one fabric square, using two strands of embroidery cotton. Position the embroidery at the right lower corner, 6 cm from the edges (one long side forms the lower edge). When the cross stitching is complete, embroider the backstitches using two strands of cotton. Along the top edge embroider a row of small block motifs: position this row 5 cm from the top edge and leave a space of three fabric squares between each block.

To finish Round the corners of both pieces on the long side below the embroidered bouquet. Fold 1 cm to the wrong side on all raw edges except top edge on each piece. Fold the top edges 4.5 cm to the wrong side. Topstitch 3 cm and then 4 cm in from the top edge, forming a casing. Stitch the side edges of the fabric together above the casing line. Sew the pieces inside the basket up to the lower stitchline of casing. Thread elastic through the casing, and secure it at the ends.

RICH RED BERRY CUSHION

SUITABLE FOR BEGINNERS

Bright red berries, white blossoms and rich greens make a striking contrast against the black fabric. This round cushion will fit happily into traditional or modern interiors. Easy stitching makes this a good project for beginners.

CUSHION WITH WREATH

Materials

40 x 80 cm piece of black even-weave fabric with 10 fabric threads to 1 cm
DMC stranded embroidery cottons in the colours indicated on the colour key plus dark garnet red number 814
Cushion insert

Finished size   About 36 cm in diameter.
The graph is on fold-out sheet C.
See the General Instructions and Stitch Library on pages 92–6.

Method   Cut the embroidery fabric into two 40 cm squares. Using running stitch, mark a 38 cm diameter circle on one of the pieces, and indicate the centre with one horizontal and one vertical line. Following the graph, embroider the motif within the marked circle. Work in cross stitch over three fabric threads, using three strands of embroidery cotton. Start the wreath at A, 147 fabric threads away from the centre. When all cross stitching is complete, work the outlines in backstitch, using two strands of cotton.

To finish   Cut the embroidered piece on the marked line of the circle. Cut a circle the same size from the other piece of fabric. Stitch the front and back together, with right sides together, with a 1 cm wide seam allowance, leaving a generous opening. Turn the cover through. Place the insert inside the cover and slipstitch the opening closed.

FROM THE GARDEN

This pretty and useful apron is decorated with a simple border and luscious fruit from the garden. The bib border and pockets are made from hardanger fabric, and the rest of the apron in plain cotton fabric. For a finishing touch, the bib and pockets are trimmed with broderie anglaise lace.

APRON

Materials

25 x 55 cm piece of white hardanger fabric with 9 double fabric threads to 1 cm
DMC stranded embroidery cottons in the colours indicated on the colour key

1.20 m of 110 cm wide white cotton fabric
3.50 m of 4 cm wide white broderie anglaise lace

See the General Instructions and Stitch Library on pages 92–6.

Method From the hardanger fabric cut one piece for the bib measuring 22 x

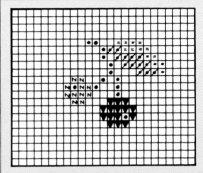

Cross stitch graphs for the apron

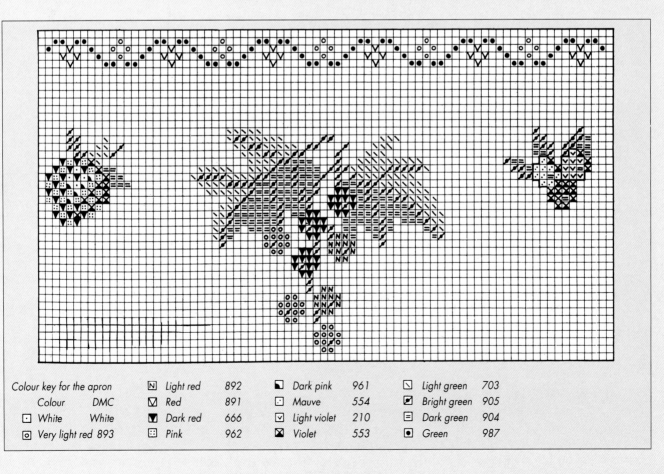

Colour key for the apron							
Colour	DMC	Ⓝ Light red	892	◼ Dark pink	961	◩ Light green	703
⊡ White	White	▽ Red	891	⊡ Mauve	554	◪ Bright green	905
⊙ Very light red	893	▼ Dark red	666	⊻ Light violet	210	⊟ Dark green	904
		⠇ Pink	962	⊠ Violet	553	⊡ Green	987

23.5 cm, and two pieces for the pockets measuring 15 x 16 cm. Following the graph, embroider the border and fruit motifs on the piece for the bib (the short side is the lower edge). Work the border over the full width of the fabric. Embroider the border and three small motifs on the pocket pieces (the long side is the lower edge). Work in cross stitch over two double fabric threads, using three strands of embroidery cotton. On all pieces, position the border 2.25 cm from the top edge. When the cross stitching is complete, work the outlines in backstitch using two strands of cotton.

Assembly From the cotton, cut one apron piece 63 x 72 cm, one bib piece 22 x 23.5 cm, two pocket pieces 15 x 16 cm, four neck ties 5 x 61 cm, and four waistband ties, two pieces 5.5 x 120 cm, and two pieces 5.5 x 70 cm. Place two neck tie pieces together, with *wrong sides* facing and 1 cm wide seam allowances turned in. Sew together, shaping one short end into a point. Repeat for other two neck tie pieces. Place the bib pieces (one embroidered and one cotton) together with *wrong sides* facing and 1 cm wide seam allowances turned in. Insert the two ties between the top edges and insert the gathered broderie anglaise lace between the top and side edges. Sew together.

For the pockets, place one embroidered and one cotton piece together with *wrong sides* facing and 1 cm wide seam allowances turned in, rounding the corners. Insert the gathered broderie anglaise lace between the outer edges and sew together. Finish the two short sides and one long side of the apron piece with a narrow hem. Sew the pockets on the apron.

Gather the top edge of the apron to measure 42 cm. Sew two waistband ties together to form a strip 188 cm long; repeat for remaining two ties. (The bands are uneven lengths so that the seam does not fall at centre front.) Place the waistband ties together with wrong sides facing and 1 cm wide seam allowance turned in. Insert the bib between the top edges and the gathered apron piece between the bottom edges. Sew together, shaping the tie ends into a point.

CLASSIC ROSES

*E*mbroider a classic rose design on a cover for an address book. The motif is worked in petit point, and a delicate border in backstitch adds the perfect finishing touch for this delightful project.

Materials

19 x 37 cm piece of ecru linen 10 or 11
DMC stranded embroidery cottons in the colours indicated on the colour key (foldout sheet A), plus medium rose number 899
Lining 19 x 37 cm piece of ecru cotton

Finished size Cover 12.5 x 17 cm. Embroidery about 8.5 x 13 cm.
The graph is on foldout sheet A.
See the General Instructions and Stitch Library on pages 92–6.

Method Following the graph, embroider the motif in continental stitch. Work each stitch over one fabric thread, using two strands of embroidery cotton. Each stitch will lie diagonally over two fabric threads at the back (see Stitch Library). Position the motif 3.25 cm from the right edge and 8 cm from the lower edge (one short side). When the motif is completed, embroider a 16.75 x 24.5 cm frame around it in backstitch. Work the stitches over two fabric threads using two strands of medium rose number 899.

To finish With right sides facing and making a 1 cm wide seam, stitch the two pieces together, leaving a small opening on one short side for turning. Cut the seam corners diagonally, turn through, and slipstitch the opening closed. Fold both short sides 4.5 cm towards the middle and hand sew in place along the top and bottom edges. Place the book inside the cover.

BLUE AND WHITE CHINA

*T*his miniature china cupboard is a
most enjoyable embroidery project. Jugs,
trays, coffee pot and teapot are all represented in cross stitch. Embroidered in only
Delft blue, white and grey, their delicate shades combine beautifully with the
colourful baskets and flower pots to form a cosy scene.

PICTURE

Materials

50 x 55 cm piece of white linen 11
DMC stranded embroidery cottons
in the colours indicated on the
colour key
A matching frame

Finished size Framed picture 27 x
35 cm.
The cross stitch graph is on foldout sheet A.
See the General Instructions and Stitch
Library on pages 92–6.

Method Following the graph,
embroider the motif on the linen. Work
in cross stitch over two fabric threads

using two strands of embroidery cotton.
Start in the right lower corner with the
bottom row of the basket, 13 cm inside
the edges. When the cross stitching is
complete, work the outlines in backstitch
using one strand of cotton.

To finish Frame the completed
embroidery as desired.

DUCKS AND GEESE

Who could resist these two cute pinafore dresses? Mother duck swims happily on the yoke of the red dress, while one of her offspring bobs blissfully away on the pocket. The blue pinafore is closed with handy shoulder ties, and is decorated with five friendly geese. The dresses will fit 2 to 3-year-olds.

RED-CHECKED DRESS

Materials

60 cm of 140 cm wide red and white checked cotton fabric
3 buttons
6 x 25 cm piece of 10 count waste canvas (10 stitches to 1 inch)
DMC stranded embroidery cottons in the colours indicated on the colour key

Size To fit 92 and 98 cm height; chest measurement 54 and 56 cm.
See the General Instructions and Stitch Library on pages 92–6.

Method Enlarge the paper pattern graph and cut out the paper patterns. Following the lines marked on the back and front yokes, make separate patterns for the neck and armhole facings. Fold the front yoke pattern open, and outline it on the fabric with running stitches, and cut out liberally. From the waste canvas cut a piece 5 x 6 cm for the pocket embroidery. Baste the remaining waste canvas over the right side of the front yoke. Following the graph, embroider the duck motif in cross stitch. Work each cross, through both layers, over two canvas threads, using three strands of embroidery cotton. Keep the needle perpendicular to the canvas while working, and stitch only through the canvas holes, not the canvas threads. Start the embroidery with the mother duck at A, 9 cm from the left side and about 2.5 cm from the lower edge of the front yoke. Embroider six or seven more ducklings. When complete, remove the basting and canvas threads one by one with tweezers. Cut out the front yoke adding 1 cm wide seam allowances.

Cut out the following fabric pieces, adding 1 cm wide seam allowances: the front yoke facings once on the fabric fold; two back yokes, two back yoke facings and two armhole facings. Cut also one skirt 34 (37) x 116 (120) cm, and one pocket 11 x 13 cm.

Assembly Stitch all pieces together with right sides together and making 1 cm wide seams. Join the side and shoulder seams of the front and back yokes. Join the shoulder seams of the

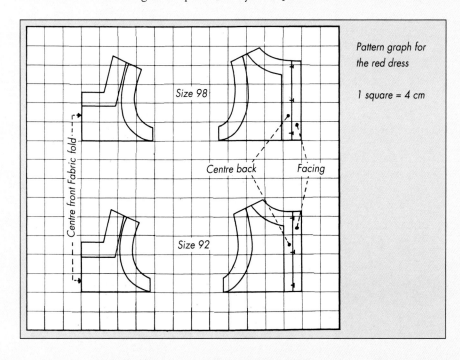

Centre front Fabric fold

Size 98

Centre back   Facing

Size 92

Pattern graph for the red dress

1 square = 4 cm

yoke facing around the split fold so it is against the inside of the skirt. Stitch the facings against the side and shoulder seams.

Make a 2 cm wide hem with 5 mm turned under on the top edge of the pocket. Embroider a small duck motif on the pocket in the same way as for the yoke. Turn the raw edges of the pocket to the wrong side and sew pocket onto the left side of the skirt front, about 7 cm from the top edge. Make a 3 cm wide hem on the lower edge of the dress. Make buttonholes in the left back yoke at the places marked. Sew buttons in matching positions on the right back yoke.

BLUE-CHECKED DRESS

Materials

55 cm of 140 cm wide blue and white checked cotton
2 buttons
6 x 20 cm piece of 12 count waste canvas (12 stitches to 1 inch)
DMC stranded embroidery cottons in the colours indicated on the colour key

Size To fit 92 and 98 cm height; chest measurement 54 and 56 cm.

front and back yoke facings. Place the facing on the right side of the yoke and sew along the back and neck edges. Clip the seam corners and turn the facing to the wrong side. Join the side and shoulder seams of the armhole facings. Sew the facings on the right side along the armholes. Clip the seam curves and turn the facings to the wrong side.

Sew the centre back seam of the skirt, leaving 8 cm open at the top for the split. Press the split seams under. Gather the top edge of the skirt to fit the yoke. Sew the skirt to the yoke, turning the back

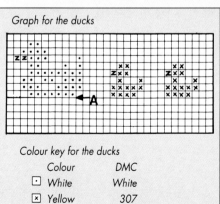

Graph for the ducks

Colour key for the ducks

	Colour	DMC
·	White	White
x	Yellow	307
z	Orange	972

canvas holes, not the canvas threads. Start the embroidery at M, on the centre front line and 1.5 cm from the lower edge of the yoke. Embroider a total of five geese. When complete, remove the basting and canvas threads one by one with tweezers.

Cut out the embroidered yoke, adding 1 cm wide seam allowances. Cut one more yoke on the fabric fold, adding 1 cm wide seam allowances. Cut four ties 5 x 42 cm and one skirt 34 (37) x 117 (120) cm.

Assembly Stitch all pieces together with right sides facing and making 1 cm wide seams. Sew each tie in half across its width, leaving the ends open, and press the seam towards the centre at the back. Close one short side on each and turn the ties right side out. Join the yokes with right sides together and with the ties placed between them at the marked places, leaving the lower edge open between the facing lines. Clip the seam curves and turn the yoke right side out. Sew the centre back seam of the skirt, leaving 11 cm open at the top for the split. Press the split seams to the wrong side. Gather the top edge of the skirt to fit the yoke. Sew the outer yoke to the skirt. Turn in the bottom edge of the yoke lining and hem against the skirt top. Sew a 3 cm wide hem on the lower edge of the dress. Make the buttonholes in the left back yoke at the places marked. Sew buttons in matching positions on the right back yoke.

See the General Instructions and Stitch Library on pages 92–6.

Method Enlarge the pattern graph and cut out the paper pattern on the fold. Open the pattern, which is the front and back yoke in one piece. Using running stitches, outline the pattern on the fabric, and mark the centre front line. Cut out liberally. Baste the waste canvas onto the right side of the front yoke. Following the graph, embroider the goose motif in cross stitch. Work each cross, through both layers, over two canvas threads, using two strands of embroidery cotton. Keep the needle perpendicular to the canvas while working, and stitch only through the

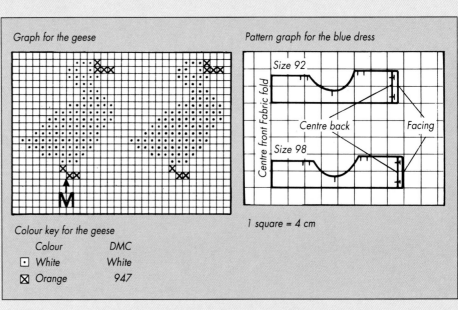

Graph for the geese

Pattern graph for the blue dress

Centre front Fabric fold

Size 92

Centre back   Facing

Size 98

1 square = 4 cm

Colour key for the geese

Colour	DMC
⊡ White	White
☒ Orange	947

SWEET FRAGRANCE

*M*ake a deliciously scented and pretty gift for a friend. Lavender bags for the wardrobe or drawers are always welcome, and these delicate little pansies will make a very special sachet. Finish with a pretty ribbon to match.

LAVENDER BAG

Materials

30 x 40 cm piece of white linen 10 DMC stranded embroidery cottons in the colours indicated on the colour key, and also dark cranberry 601, medium blue 826, and medium burnt orange 946
50 cm of narrow green ribbon
Dried lavender

Finished size About 10 x 16 cm. See the General Instructions and Stitch Library on pages 92–6.

Method From linen cut two pieces 20 x 30 cm. Following the graph, embroider the motif on one piece of linen. Work in cross stitch over two fabric threads using two strands of embroidery cotton. Position the motif in the centre and 6.5 cm from the lower edge (one short side). When the cross stitching is complete, work the outlines in backstitch using two strands of cotton. When the embroidery is complete, cut the sides and lower edges of the fabric to 2.5 cm, and the top edge 8.5 cm from the embroidery. Cut the other piece of linen to the same size.

With right sides facing, sew the sides and lower edge of the pieces together, making a 1 cm wide seam. Withdraw five fabric threads along the top edge, 6 cm from the top edge. Baste a 2 cm wide double hem along the top. Using one strand of white embroidery cotton, work the open border in ladder hemstitch over three fabric threads. Secure the hem when making the second row of ladder hemstitch. Work this row exactly the same as the first one.

To finish Thread the ribbon through the open border, fill the bag with lavender, and tie the ribbon into a bow at the front.

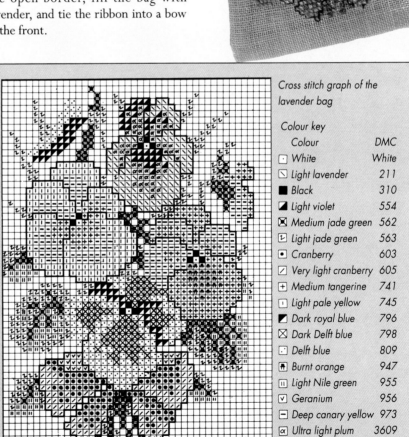

Cross stitch graph of the lavender bag

Colour key

Colour	DMC
⊡ White	White
◲ Light lavender	211
■ Black	310
◣ Light violet	554
⊠ Medium jade green	562
Ⴑ Light jade green	563
⊡ Cranberry	603
☑ Very light cranberry	605
✚ Medium tangerine	741
⊡ Light pale yellow	745
◪ Dark royal blue	796
⊠ Dark Delft blue	798
⊡ Delft blue	809
⊞ Burnt orange	947
⊪ Light Nile green	955
☑ Geranium	956
⊟ Deep canary yellow	973
⊠ Ultra light plum	3609

Outlines *Around the yellow-orange pansies in medium burnt orange 946; around the blue pansy in medium blue 826; around the purple pansy and pink bow in dark cranberry 601.*

67

A WREATH OF FLOWERS

*H*ere's a collection of small bags and cases that are quick and easy to make. The comb, a compact, mirror and glasses cases, and pretty toilet bag would be perfect gifts. The pastel flowers on black fabric look stunning, especially with the finishing touch of contrast bindings.

TOILET BAG WITH FLOWER WREATH

Materials

25 x 40 cm piece of black evenweave fabric with 10 fabric threads to 1 cm
DMC stranded embroidery cottons in the colours indicated on the colour key
15 cm black zipper
1 m pink bias binding
Heavyweight black interfacing
Lining 25 x 40 cm floral cotton fabric

Assembly With wrong sides together, baste the outer fabric and lining pieces of each of the two gussets together. Finish one short edge (the top edge) of each gusset with bias binding. Round the corners of the lower side of each gusset. With *wrong sides* together, and matching the centre of the long sides, baste the embroidered and lining pieces of the bag together. Fold a 2.5 cm wide hem to the wrong side along the short edges. Turn under 1.5 cm of the lining fabric and stitch to the hem of the embroidered fabric, forming a black border. With *wrong sides* together, sew the left gusset between the bag sides with a 5 mm wide seam; position the centre of the lower side of the gusset onto the centre of the left long side of the bag, leaving 1.5 cm open at the top. Finish the seams of the complete left side with pink bias binding, turning the raw edges in at the top.

Sew the zipper to the top edge, with the closed part on the side of the left gusset. Sew the remaining gusset between the right sides of the bag in the same way as for the left gusset. Sew a 10 cm long piece of bias binding together across its width with the short ends turned inwards. Knot it around the zipper tag.

Finished size About 17 x 15.5 cm. The motif measures about 9.5 cm in diameter.
See the General Instructions and Stitch Library on pages 92–6.

Method From the embroidery fabric cut one piece 17 x 39 cm, and two strips 3 x 15 cm for the gussets. Following the graph, embroider the motif on the large piece. Work in cross stitch over two fabric threads, using two strands of embroidery cotton. Start at M, 15.5 cm down from the top edge (one short side), and position the motif in the centre. From both the interfacing and the lining fabric, cut one piece 17 x 34 cm and two strips 3 x 15 cm.

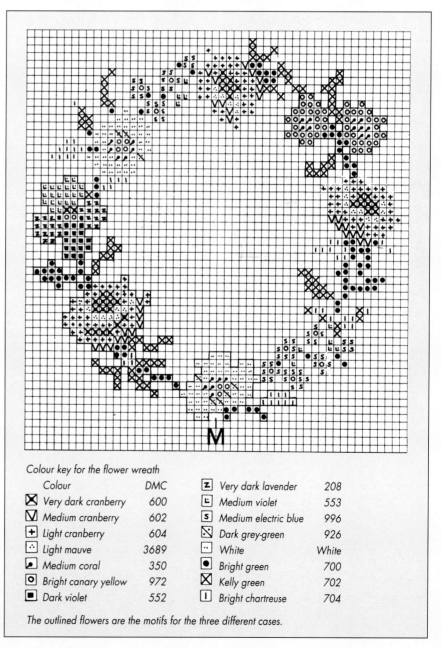

Colour key for the flower wreath

	Colour	DMC
☒	Very dark cranberry	600
Ⓥ	Medium cranberry	602
⊞	Light cranberry	604
⋰	Light mauve	3689
◢	Medium coral	350
Ⓞ	Bright canary yellow	972
▣	Dark violet	552

	Colour	DMC
☒	Very dark lavender	208
Ⓛ	Medium violet	553
Ⓢ	Medium electric blue	996
◩	Dark grey-green	926
⋰	White	White
●	Bright green	700
☒	Kelly green	702
Ⅰ	Bright chartreuse	704

The outlined flowers are the motifs for the three different cases.

without seam allowance, from the embroidered piece: ensure that the motif is positioned in the centre, 4.5 cm up from the lower edge. Cut A also from the interfacing and the lining fabric without seam.

Assembly Place the three layers of the front and the three layers of the back together with *wrong sides* facing. Finish the straight top edge of A with bias binding. Pin A on top of A+B with *wrong sides* facing and finish the case all around with bias binding. Sew on a snap fastener to close the flap.

COMB CASE

Materials

15 x 25 cm piece of black evenweave fabric with 10 fabric threads to 1 cm
DMC stranded embroidery cottons in the colours indicated on the colour key
45 cm green bias binding
Lining 15 x 25 cm piece of black and white dotted cotton fabric

Finished size About 6.5 x 20 cm. See the General Instructions and Stitch Library on pages 92–6.

Method Enlarge the pattern graph and cut out the pattern piece in paper. Using running stitch, outline the shape of the case on the embroidery fabric. Following the graph for the toilet bag, embroider the white flower (at lower centre) over the front section of the case. Work in cross stitch over two fabric threads using two strands of thread. Start at M, and position the motif 4 cm from the right side edge and 3.5 cm from the lower edge.

Using embroidery cotton number 702, add an extra leaf pointing downwards; work this in the same way as the leaf worked in number 704.

Cut the embroidered fabric on the marked outline. Cut the pattern of the case once from the lining fabric.

Assembly Place the fabric pieces together, with *wrong sides* facing. Sew the

GLASSES CASE

Materials

25 cm square piece of black evenweave fabric, with 10 fabric threads to 1 cm
DMC stranded embroidery cottons in the colours indicated on the colour key
Lining 25 cm square of floral cotton fabric
Heavyweight black interfacing
A snap fastener
75 cm mauve bias binding

Finished size About 9 x 18 cm. See the General Instructions and Stitch Library on pages 92–6.

Method Cut the embroidery fabric into two pieces, each 12.5 cm x 25 cm. Following the graph for the toilet bag,

embroider the pansy (on the left) on one of the pieces. Work in cross stitch over two fabric threads using two strands of embroidery cotton. Start with the base of the stem, and position the motif 7 cm from the lower edge and 5.5 cm from the right side edge (one long side).

Enlarge the pattern graph and cut out the pattern piece. Cut A+B (the back of the case + flap) without seam allowance from the plain piece of embroidery fabric, the interfacing and the lining fabric. Cut A (front of case) separately,

Pattern graph for the glasses case

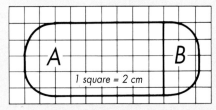

1 square = 2 cm

bias binding to the right side of the fabric from A to B to C. Secure the bias binding by hand from A to B on the inside. Fold the case in half with A on top of B. Slip the side of the case without bias binding underneath the open bias binding, and secure it from A–B to C.

CASE FOR POWDER COMPACT OR MIRROR

Materials

15 x 30 cm piece of black evenweave material with 10 fabric threads to 1 cm
DMC stranded embroidery cottons in the colours indicated on the colour key
Heavyweight black interfacing
Lining 15 x 30 cm piece of cotton fabric

Finished size Powder compact case about 9 cm in diameter; mirror case about 10.5 cm in diameter.

See the General Instructions and Stitch Library on pages 92–6.

Method Using running stitch, outline a 9 cm or 10.5 cm diameter circle on the evenweave fabric. Following the graph for the toilet bag, embroider the pink flower (lower left) or yellow flower (top right) in the centre of the outlined circle. Work in cross stitch over two fabric threads using two strands of embroidery cotton. When all embroidery is complete, cut out the outlined circle, adding a 1 cm wide seam allowance. Cut one more circle the same size from evenweave fabric, and two from the lining fabric. Cut two 9 cm or 10.5 cm diameter circles from interfacing.

Assembly Baste the interfacing to the back of the embroidery fabric pieces. Sew the lining and reinforced pieces together with right sides facing, leaving a small opening for turning. Trim

and clip the seams. Turn each piece right side out and slipstitch the opening closed. With the lined sides together, baste the two circles together, and hand sew the outer edges together a little more than halfway around. Decorate the open fabric edges with blanket stitch, using two strands of number 602 or 972 embroidery thread.

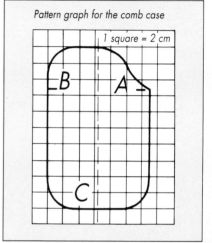

Pattern graph for the comb case

1 square = 2 cm

B   A

C

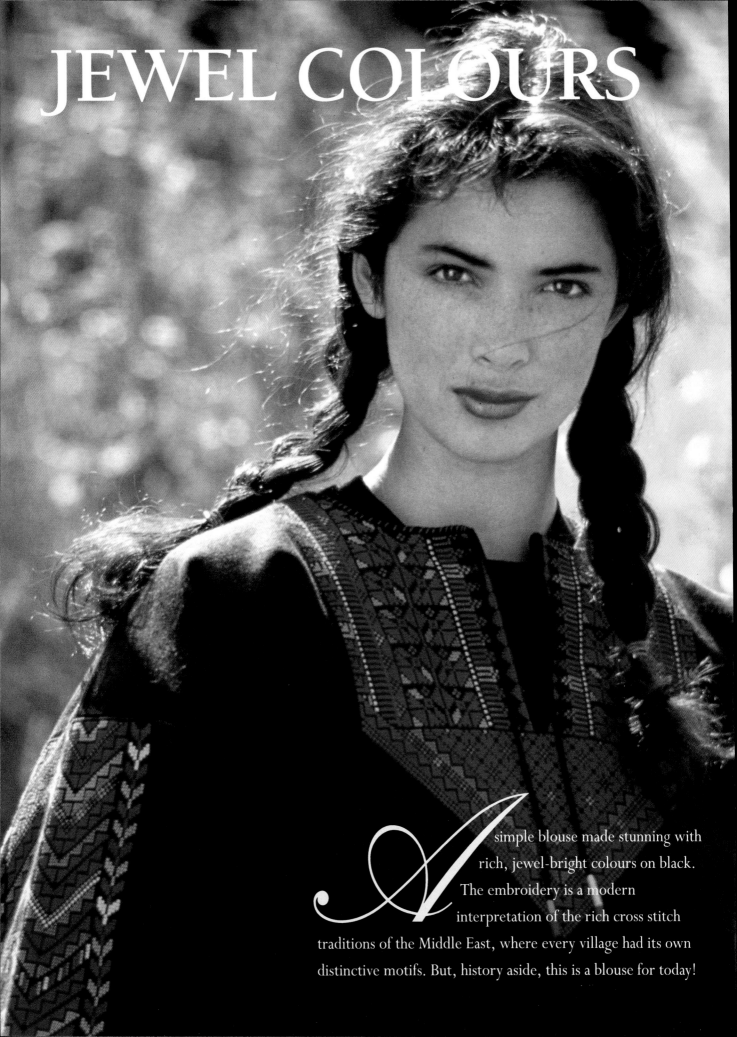

JEWEL COLOURS

A simple blouse made stunning with rich, jewel-bright colours on black. The embroidery is a modern interpretation of the rich cross stitch traditions of the Middle East, where every village had its own distinctive motifs. But, history aside, this is a blouse for today!

Pattern graph of black blouse

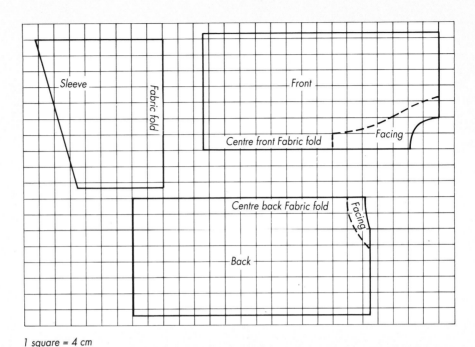

Sleeve

Fabric fold

Front

Centre front Fabric fold

Facing

Centre back Fabric fold

Facing

Back

1 square = 4 cm

BLACK BLOUSE

Materials

1.35 m of 140 cm wide
evenweave embroidery fabric with
10 threads to 1 cm
DMC stranded embroidery cottons
in the colours indicated on the
colour key
1.10 m black cotton cord

Finished size To fit medium size.
The graph is on foldout sheet C.
See the General Instructions and Stitch
Library on pages 92–6.

Method Enlarge the pattern graph of
the blouse and cut out the paper patterns.
Use running stitches to outline the front
and the sleeves on the fabric. Use a
vertical line of running stitches to mark
the centre front line on the front, and the
centre of the sleeves. Following the
graph, embroider the motifs in cross
stitch. Work the crosses over two fabric
threads, using two strands of cotton.

To embroider the front, start at M,
exactly on the marked centre front line,
about 25 cm down from the marked
neckline. Work the motif in reverse for

the right side of the front. To embroider
sleeves, work the motif 1 cm from the
top edge, matching the centre with the
marked line. When the embroidery is
complete, cut the pieces, adding 1 cm

wide seam and 4 cm wide hem
allowances. Cut the neck facings once
from black fabric, adding 1 cm wide seam
allowances.

Assembly Join all pieces with right
sides together, making 1 cm wide
seams. Stitch the shoulder seams. Sew
the underarm sleeve seams. Sew the
sleeves into the armholes, placing the
centre of the sleeves against the
shoulder seams. Stitch the side seams.
Stitch the shoulder seams of the facings.
Sew the facing exactly along the
embroidered border of the front and
back neckline, and along the split. Slash
the centre front line to about 1 cm
above the embroidery, and cut the seam
diagonally to the stitching line. Clip the
neck seams to the stitchline. Turn the
facing to the wrong side.

To finish Using red embroidery cotton
number 666, secure the cord with
overcast stitches onto the neckline,
matching the centre of the cord with the
centre back. Wind the ends of the cord
with different colours of stranded cotton.
Make a 2 cm wide double hem along the
lower edge of the blouse and the sleeves.

BREAKFAST IN BED

T hese cheerful blue gentians are sure to brighten up your bedroom and give a
personal touch to a purchased sheet or quilt set.. Embroide them on a cotton band,
and sew it over fresh, blue and white striped cotton pillowcases. And if the motif
is used to decorate a pretty tray cloth, breakfast in bed will turn into an even bigger
treat. To complete the picture, a floral border will transform a simple towel into
something special!

QUILT OR SHEET SET

Materials

One double bed blue and white striped quilt set, or one double bed blue and white striped sheet set with pillow cases as well as a white sheet
8 x 1.60 cm piece of white hardanger fabric with 9 double fabric threads to 1 cm
DMC stranded embroidery cottons in the colours indicated on the colour key on foldout sheet F
Snap fasteners

Finished size Pillow case about 60 x 70 cm. Width of border about 6 cm.
The graph is on foldout sheet F.
See the General Instructions and Stitch Library on pages 92–6.

Pillow cases Cut the fabric strip into two pieces measuring 8 x 80 cm, and embroider a border of flowers on each piece in the same way as described for the towel border. Stitch the strips 10 cm from the top edge on each pillow case, with all the raw edges turned under (1 cm wide seam allowance at top and bottom); the right edge at the fold of the pillow case, the left edge on the flap.

Quilt set Sew the white and striped sheets together to form a quilt cover, and finish with snap fasteners at the end.

TOWEL BORDER

Materials

Blue and white striped towel
About 8 cm wide piece of white hardanger fabric with 9 double fabric threads to 1 cm in the desired length, plus 5 cm for hems
DMC stranded embroidery cottons in the colours indicated on the colour key on foldout sheet F

Finished size Width of border about 6 cm.
The graph is on foldout sheet F.
See the General Instructions and Stitch Library on pages 92–6.

Method Following the graph, work the motif in cross stitch over the centre of the fabric. Work each cross over *two* double fabric threads, using three strands of embroidery cotton. Start the embroidery at A, and repeat the motif marked 'Repeat' the desired length.

To finish Pin the embroidered band onto the towel. Turn the raw edges along top, bottom and ends to the wrong side (1 cm wide seam allowance at top and bottom) and stitch the piece in position.

TRAY CLOTH

Materials

70 cm square piece white hardanger fabric with 9 double fabric threads to 1 cm
DMC stranded embroidery cottons in the colours indicated on the colour key on foldout sheet F

Finished size 56 cm square.
Embroidered border is about 7 cm wide.
The graph is on foldout sheet F.
See the General Instructions and Stitch Library on pages 92–6.

Method Make one vertical and one horizontal line in running stitches to indicate the centre of the fabric. Following the graph, embroider the motif in cross stitch. Work each cross over two double fabric threads using three strands embroidery cotton. Start the embroidery at M, 221 double fabric threads away from the centre. Work the motif marked 'Repeat' a total of three times to complete one side of the border. Embroider the same border on the three remaining sides of the cloth. Refer also to the photograph of the completed piece for guidance.

To finish Remove the eighth double fabric thread to the corners, above and also below the embroidered border. Weave the short ends of the threads back into the fabric. Work the open border above the embroidery in ladder hemstitch, which is worked in the same way as open hemstitch, but on both sides of the open border (see the Stitch Library). Work each stitch over two double fabric threads, using one strand of number 800 embroidery cotton.

Baste a 2.5 cm wide double hem around the cloth, making mitred corners. Secure the hem with ladder hemstitch exactly below the remaining open border.

BLUSHING APPLES

*T*wo blushing apples decorate this pair of attractive cushions. The fine linen and stitchery are complemented by the elegant flat finish. The autumn tones and delicate shading in these two designs will make them a pleasure to stitch.

CUSHIONS

Materials

For one cushion
46 x 92 cm piece of ecru linen 11
DMC stranded embroidery cottons in the colours indicated on the colour key
A 35 cm square cushion insert

Finished size 43 cm square.
See the General Instructions and Stitch Library on pages 91–5.

Method Cut the linen into two 46 cm squares. Following the graph, embroider the selected motif in cross stitch in the centre of one piece of linen. Work each cross over two fabric threads, using two strands of embroidery cotton: each square on the graph represents four crosses. When the cross stitching is complete, work the outlines in backstitch in the colours indicated on the graph, using one strand of cotton.

Around the motif, embroider a 32 cm square in backstitch, using two strands of cotton in number 471 or number 402.

To finish With right sides together and making a 1.5 cm wide seam, stitch the front and back together along four corners and three sides. Cut away the seam corners and pull the cover through. Put the insert inside the cover and slipstitch the opening closed. Sew a row of topstitching around the cushion, 1.5 cm away from the embroidered frame: sew through the cover only, not the cushion insert.

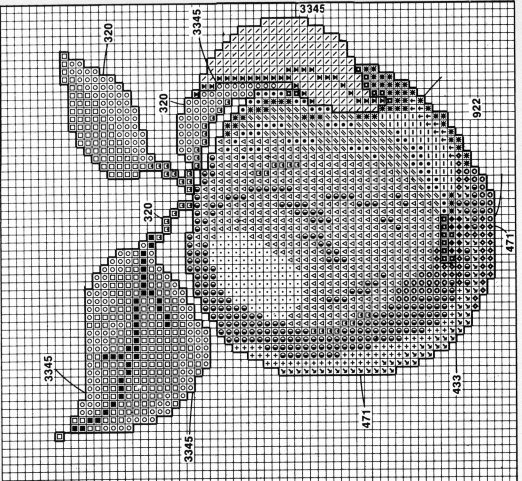

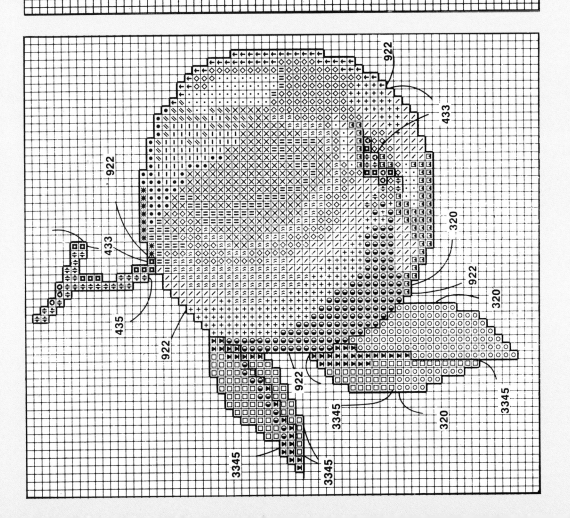

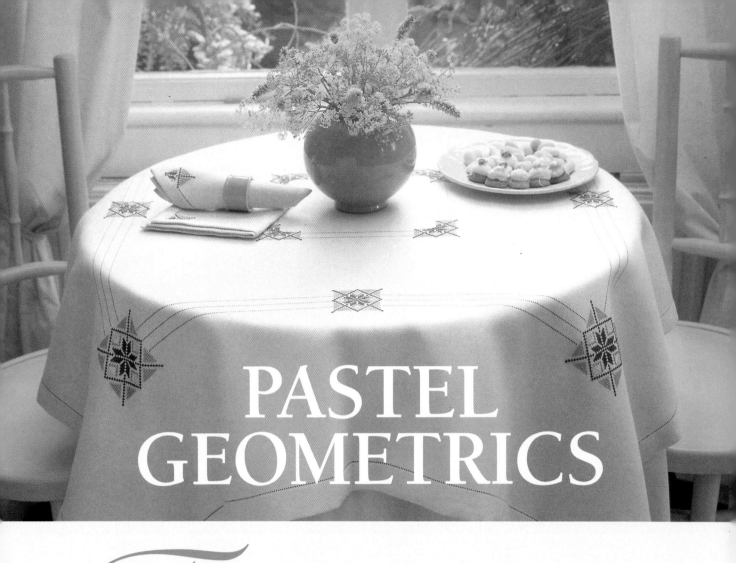

PASTEL GEOMETRICS

*T*his pastel pink tablecloth with matching serviettes shows that it can be fun to play with a motif: work it large, small and just in parts. The motifs are connected with woven lines in red embroidery cotton. For the teacosy, select pastel yellow hardanger. If the colours are hard to find, dye the fabric yourself.

PINK TABLECLOTH

Materials

1.25 m of 150 cm wide pale pink hardanger fabric with 9 double fabric threads to 1 cm
DMC stranded embroidery cottons in the colours indicated on the colour key
DMC broder cotton number 16 in red, number 321.

Finished size About 108 cm square. See the General Instructions and Stitch Library on pages 92–6.

Method Mark the centre of the cloth with one horizontal and one vertical line in running stitches. Using running stitches, mark in the centre of the cloth one 25 cm square and one 68 cm square. Following the graph, embroider the various motifs in cross stitch. Work the crosses over two double fabric threads, using three strands of embroidery cotton.

Work the inner square as follows: stay *within* the marked line, and embroider Motif 1 once in each corner. Position the extending red crosses against the marked line. Connect the motifs as follows: as indicated on the graph, remove between the motifs one double fabric thread twice, twelve double fabric threads apart. Darn the short ends of the fabric threads back into the motifs at the back. Weave a length of red broder cotton through the open lines, replacing the fabric threads.

Work the outer square as follows: stay *within* the marked line, and embroider Motif 2 once in each corner. Position the extended red crosses against the marked line. When completed, embroider Motif 3 between each corner motif. Position these in the centre of the marked horizontal or vertical line, placing their centre in line with the

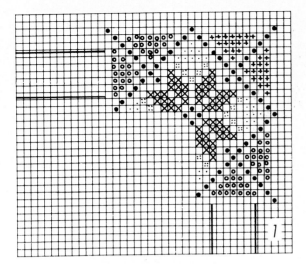

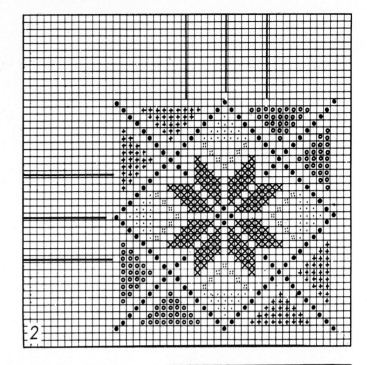

centre of the corner motifs. Connect the motifs as follows: as indicated on the graph for motif 2, remove between the motifs one double fabric thread three times, eleven double fabric threads apart. Darn the short ends of the fabric threads back into the motifs at the back. Weave lengths of red broder cotton through the open lines, replacing the fabric threads.

At a distance of 20 cm from the outer embroidered border, baste a 3 cm double hem, making mitred corners. Embroider motif 4 (there are two graphs for motif 4, each with a different colour) on each corner above the hem, alternating the motifs. Position the two outer red crosses exactly against the hem. As indicated on the graph, remove one double fabric thread above the hem up to the motifs, and darn the short ends of the threads back into the motifs at the back. Weave red broder cotton through the open lines, replacing the fabric threads. Sew the hem in place.

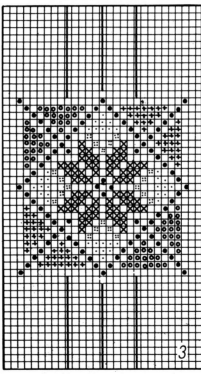

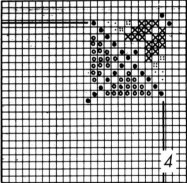

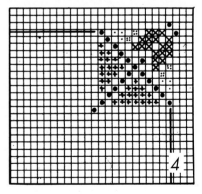

SERVIETTES

Materials

For one serviette 36 cm square pale pink hardanger fabric with 9 double fabric threads to 1 cm DMC stranded embroidery cottons in the colours indicated on the graph for the tablecloth
DMC broder cotton number 16 in red, number 321

Finished size About 30 cm square. See the General Instructions and Stitch Library on pages 92–6.

Method Hem the serviette with a 1.5 cm double hem, making mitred corners. Embroider motif 4 on one corner, exactly above the hem. Work this in the same way as described for the tablecloth.

Colour key for Pastel geometrics tablecloth, serviettes and teacosy

	Colour	DMC
⊠	Pewter grey	317
◎	Sky blue	519
⦂	Light aquamarine	993
●	Christmas red	321
▫	Light lemon	445
⊞	Pale geranium pink	957

Enlarge the graph for the cosy pattern and cut out the paper pattern. Cut the pattern once from each embroidered piece, adding a 1 cm wide seam and a 9 cm hem allowance; place the lower edge of the motifs 4 cm from the pattern line. Stitch the two pieces together with right sides facing and make a 1 cm wide seam, leaving the lower edge open. Turn the cover right side out.

TEACOSY

Materials

45 x 100 cm pale yellow hardanger fabric with 9 double fabric threads to 1 cm
DMC stranded embroidery cottons in the colours indicated on the colour key for the tablecloth
DMC broder cotton number 16 in red number 321
70 cm of 90 cm wide cotton fabric for the inner cosy
Synthetic fibrefill

Note If you prefer, select white hardanger, and dye the fabric with Dylon hot-water dye in colour number 2.

Finished size 3 0 x 42 cm
See the General Instructions and Stitch Library on pages 92–6.

Method Cut the hardanger into two 45 x 50 cm pieces. Following the graph for the tablecloth, embroider the motifs on both pieces. Work in cross stitch over two double fabric threads, using three strands of embroidery thread. Embroider motif 2 in the centre of each fabric piece, 15 cm from the lower edge (one long side). Then embroider motif 3 once on

each side; match the lower row of this motif with the lower row of the centre motif, and keep a distance of 7.75 cm between the red corner crosses.

Following the graph of motif 3, remove one double fabric thread three times between the motifs, eleven double fabric threads apart. Darn the short ends of the fabric threads back into the motifs at the back. Weave lengths of red broder cotton through the open lines, replacing the fabric threads.

Inner cosy Cut the cosy pattern four times from cotton fabric, adding a 1 cm wide seam allowance. Assemble two cosies in cotton, place one inside the other, wrong sides together, fill tightly, and sew the lower edges together. Place the inner cosy inside the cover. Fold the lower edge of the cover 9 cm to the wrong side and secure it with a 1 cm turning onto the inner cosy.

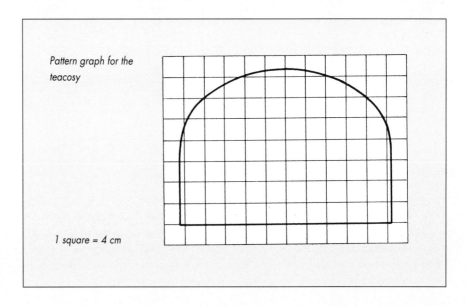

Pattern graph for the teacosy

1 square = 4 cm

EGGS FOR BREAKFAST

*K*eep those eggs warm with this delightful egg warmer. A quick and easy project, it would make a lovely gift, and even beginners will find it straightforward.

EGG WARMER

Materials

11 x 17 cm unbleached linen with 8 fabric threads per 1 cm
11 x 17 cm piece of flannel
Small amounts of DMC stranded embroidery cottons

Finished size 7.5 x 8 cm

Method Enlarge the pattern graph and cut out the paper pattern. Cut the linen and flannel fabric each into two equal pieces, measuring 11 x 8.5 cm. Mark the outline of the pattern on one piece of linen with running stitches. Following the graph, embroider the motif in cross stitch over two fabric threads, using three strands of embroidery cotton. Position the motif in the centre and 1.5 cm from the lower marked line.

To finish Cut the pattern twice from the linen and the flannel, adding a 2 cm wide hem allowance on the lower edge of the pieces of linen. Put the linen pieces together with right sides facing. Place one piece of flannel on top and one piece underneath. Stitch together on the marked line, leaving the lower edges open. Zigzag closely next to the stitch line and cut away excess seam allowance. Fold the lower 2 cm of the linen to the wrong side and sew in place.

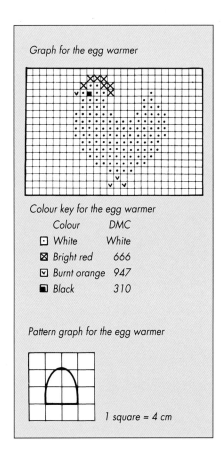

Graph for the egg warmer

Colour key for the egg warmer

	Colour	DMC
⊡	White	White
⊠	Bright red	666
☑	Burnt orange	947
■	Black	310

Pattern graph for the egg warmer

1 square = 4 cm

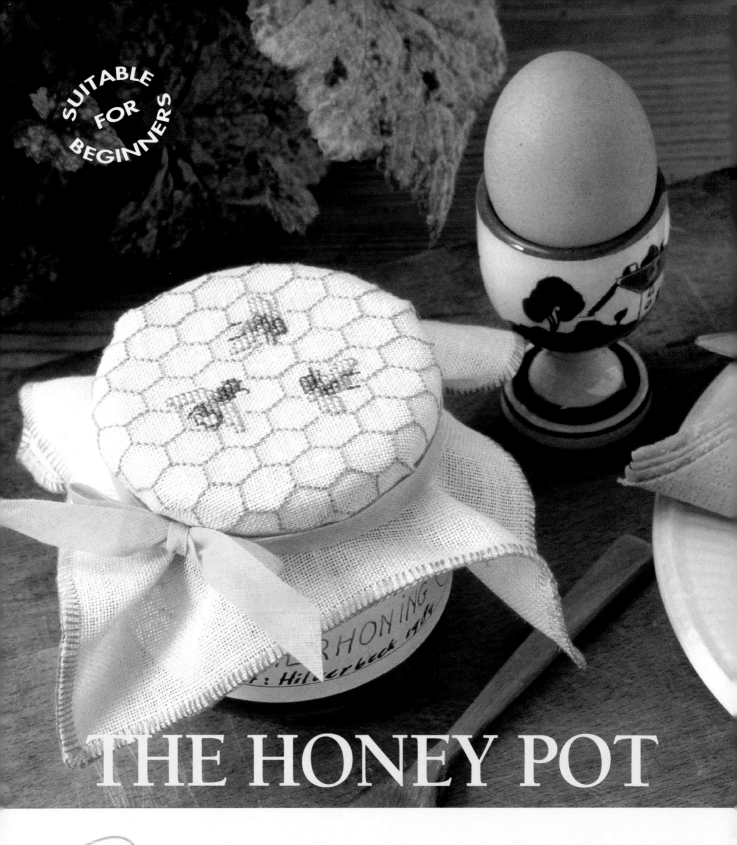

THE HONEY POT

Y ou can make a gift of honey or home-made preserves very special by embroidering a pretty lid cover for the jar. Here three busy bees on a background of honeycomb decorate a small lid cover for the honey jar. Quick and easy to make, this is a project that will suit those who are just beginning cross stitch.

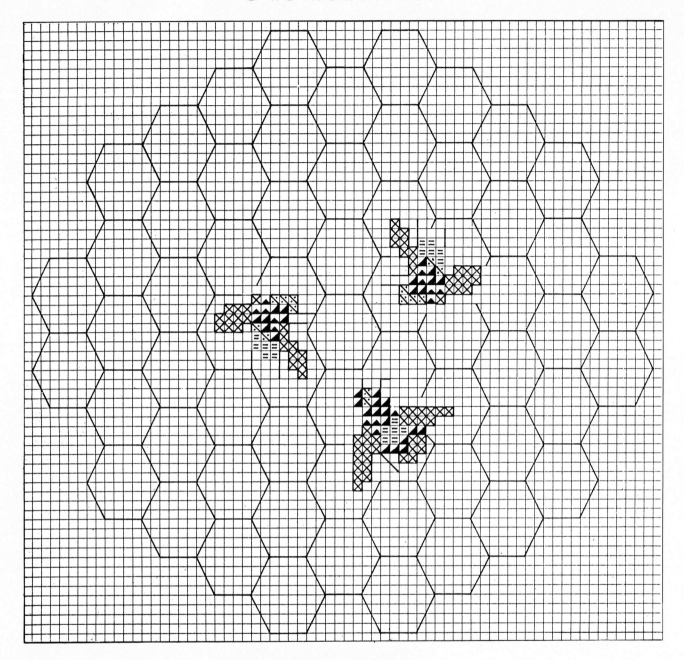

LID COVER

Materials

18 cm square piece of ecru linen 10
DMC stranded embroidery cottons in the colours indicated on the colour key, plus medium old gold number 729

Finished size 17 cm square.
See the General Instructions and Stitch Library on pages 92–6.

Method Fold the fabric edges under

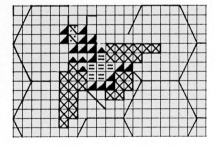

Colour key for Honey Pot lid cover		
Colour		DMC
◪ Dark drab brown		611
▤ Medium tangerine		741
⊠ Very light pearl grey		762
◰ Light steel grey		318
◩ Medium drab brown		612

5 mm, and work a row of blanket stitch around the edges. Work the stitches five fabric threads deep and two fabric threads apart, using two strands of medium old gold number 729.

Following the graph, embroider the motif in cross stitch in the centre of the fabric. Work each cross over two fabric threads, using two strands of embroidery cotton. Finally, work honeycomb in backstitch using two strands of embroidery cotton in medium old gold.

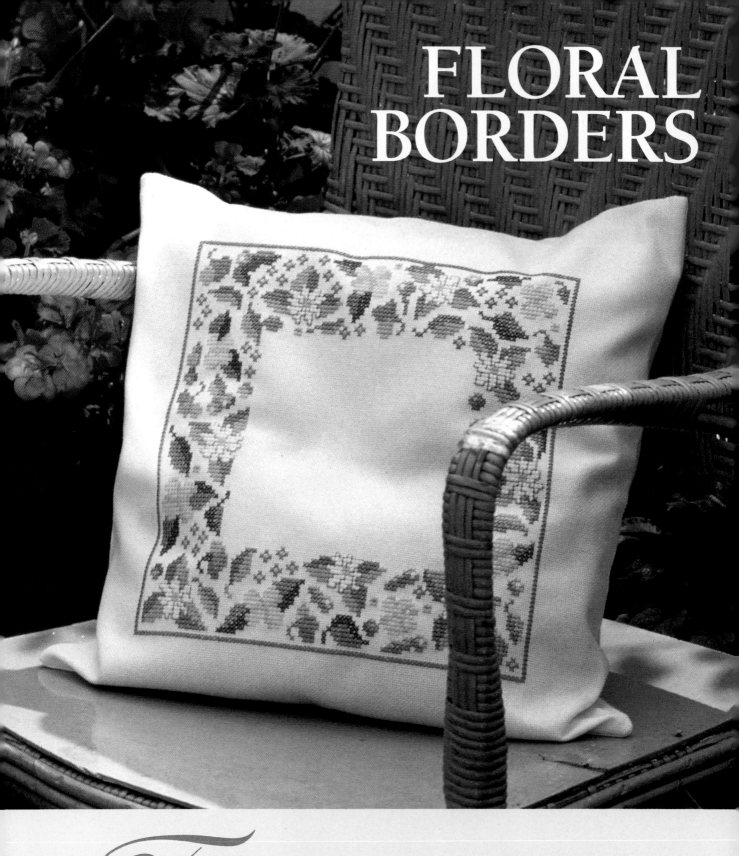

FLORAL BORDERS

These two charming borders can be used in many different ways. They would suit both a cushion and a tablecloth. Or turn a plain skirt into a stylish garment with the design embroidered on the pockets. The skirt is easy to sew and can be made to fit any size: simply adapt the waistband to the desired measurement.

CUSHION

Materials

47 cm square piece of white evenweave fabric with 7 fabric threads to 1 cm (such as Davossa, DMC article no. 3770)
47 cm square piece of white cotton fabric for the backing
DMC stranded embroidery cottons in the colours in the colour key
A 42 cm square cushion insert

Finished size Cushion is 42 cm square. Embroidery is 28 cm square. The graph is on foldout sheet F. See the General Instructions and Stitch Library on pages 92–6.

Method Following the graph, embroider the motif in cross stitch. Work each cross over two fabric threads, using three strands of embroidery cotton. Start the embroidery at the right lower corner, 9 cm from the edges. When the cross stitching is complete, work the outlines

Colour key for Floral Borders skirt

	Colour	DMC
⊞	Nile green	954
☑	Light emerald green	912
⊟	Ultra light avocado	472
⊞	Very light avocado	471
⊠	Light avocado	470
⫾⫾	Very dark parrot green	907
⫾	Light salmon	761
⊙	Salmon	760
●	Coral	351
□	Off-white	746
◱	Medium yellow	743
☑	Very light blue	827
◨	Medium electric blue	996

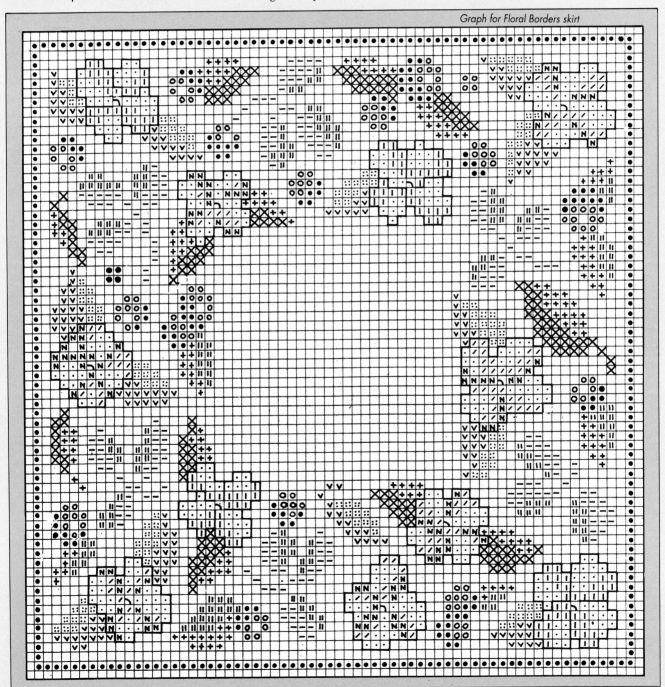

Graph for Floral Borders skirt

in backstitch, using three strands of Delft blue number 809.

To finish With right sides facing, sew the backing to the front along four corners and three sides, 7 cm away from the embroidery. Trim the seam and cut the seam corners diagonally. Turn the cover through, place the insert inside the cover, and slipstitch the opening closed.

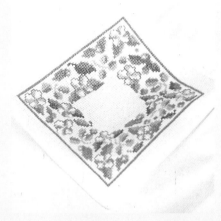

SKIRT

Materials

1.60 m of 110 cm wide white cotton fabric
5 large buttons
Fusible interfacing 7 cm wide by length of waistband
Two 28 cm square pieces of 11 count white Aida fabric
DMC stranded embroidery cottons in the colours in the colour key

Finished size Embroidery 16 cm square. See the General Instructions and Stitch Library on pages 92–6.

Note The skirt can be made to fit any size. For the waistband, measure the waist plus 6 cm for two overlaps, plus 2 cm seam allowances, and make more or fewer pleats in the skirt to fit.

Embroidery Following the graph, embroider the motif in the centre of both pieces of Aida. Work each cross over one fabric square, using three strands of embroidery cotton. Start the embroidery at the right lower corner, 5 cm from the edges. When the cross stitching is complete, work the outlines in backstitch, using three strands of medium electric blue number 996 for the blue flowers, and coral number 351 for the salmon pink flowers. When completed, cut away the lower edges and sides 3.5 cm from the embroidery, and the top edges 5.5 cm from the embroidery.

Cutting From cotton cut one piece of fabric 75 cm deep and 102 cm wide for the front skirt and two pieces 75 cm deep and 55 cm wide for the back skirt. For the waistband, cut one piece 7 cm wide in the required length.

Assembly Stitch the side seams of the skirt. Fold a 3 cm wide facing at the top edge of the pockets to the wrong side and sew in place. Stitch the pockets to the skirt with 1 cm of the raw edges turned under; position them about 17 cm from the top edge of the skirt and place them against the side seams. Fold a 6 cm wide facing to the wrong side along the side edges of the back skirt pieces. Pleat the top edge of the skirt (from centre front to centre back) to the required waist measurement. Reinforce the waistband with interfacing. With right sides together, fold the waistband in half across its width. Stitch both short ends and turn right side out. Sew the waistband to the skirt, allowing a 3 cm overlap at each end. Make a 3 cm wide hem along the lower edge of the skirt. Make a buttonhole in the waistband and make four buttonholes in the left back skirt. Sew the buttons in matching positions on the right back skirt.

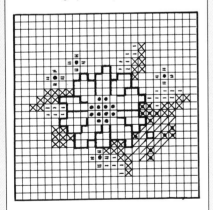

FLOWERS AT YOUR FEET

D ecorate a pair of espadrilles with a colourful flower motif. Waste canvas is used to transfer the pattern to the shoes, and the same method can be used to transfer any cross-stitch design to clothing of any fabric.

ESPADRILLES

Materials

Espadrilles
Small quantities of DMC stranded embroidery cottons in the colours listed in the colour key
2 small pieces of 10 count waste canvas (10 stitches to 1 inch)

See the General Instructions and Stitch Library on pages 92–6.

Cross stitch graph for espadrilles

Colour key for flower pattern

	Colour	DMC			
			☒	Dark pink	600
⊡	Light green	907	☑	Pink	604
☒	Dark green	905	⦿	Yellow	643
☐	White	White	⊟	Blue	797

Backstitch on the flower dark pink

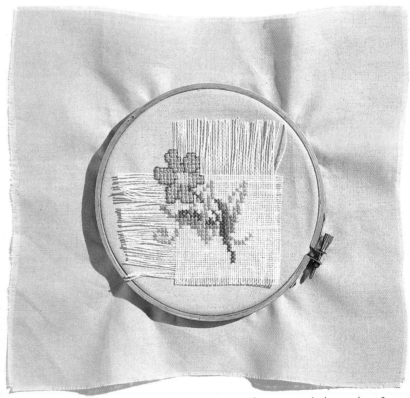

Here a scrap of linen is used instead of waste canvas. If you want to do this, use linen 8.

Method Baste the waste canvas to the espadrilles over the area to be embroidered. Following the graph, embroider the motif in cross stitch. Work each cross through both layers, over two fabric threads using four strands of embroidery cotton. Keep the needle perpendicular to the canvas while working, and stitch only through the canvas holes, not the canvas threads. When the cross stitching is complete, work the outlines in backstitch using three strands of thread. When complete, dampen the canvas and remove the basting and canvas threads one by one with tweezers. Work the motif reversed for the other espadrille.

ANEMONES IN THE ROUND

nemones in mauve, pink and red stand out beautifully fresh against the white background of this tablecloth. It is suitable for a round or square table, and is made from large-weave fabric, so the embroidery is quick and easy. The cloth and its matching serviettes are finished with red bias binding.

Method Cut the fabric into a circle of 150 cm diameter, and finish the edges with bias binding.

Mark the centre of the cloth with one horizontal and one vertical line in running stitch. Following the graph, embroider the motif in cross stitch. Work each cross over one fabric square, using five strands of embroidery cotton. When the cross stitching is complete, work the outlines in backstitch, using four strands of cotton. Start the embroidery at A, 106 fabric squares away from the centre. To complete the design, repeat the motif three more times.

SERVIETTES

Materials

For one serviette
41 cm square piece of white Herta fabric (DMC article number 3611)
DMC stranded embroidery cottons in the colours indicated on the colour key
About 1.70 m of 1 cm wide red bias binding

Finished size 41 cm square.
See General Instructions and Stitch Library on pages 92–6.

Method Finish the raw edges of the fabric with bias binding. Following the graph, embroider the motif in cross stitch. Work the crosses over one fabric square, using five strands of embroidery cotton (the flower either in lavender or cranberry). When the cross stitching is complete, work the outlines in backstitch, using four strands of cotton. Position the motif at a corner of the serviette, about thirteen fabric squares in from the bias binding.

TABLECLOTH

Materials

1.60 m of 170 cm wide white Herta fabric (DMC article number 3611)
DMC stranded embroidery cottons in the colours in the colour key
About 5.50 m of 2 cm wide red bias binding

Finished size The tablecloth is 150 cm in diameter. The embroidered wreath measures 89 cm in diameter.
The graph is on foldout sheet E.
See the General Instructions and Stitch Library on pages 92–6.

Outlines *Very dark violet number 550 around the lavender flower; medium cranberry number 602 around the cranberry flower.*

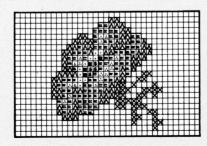

Colour key for the serviettes

Colour		DMC
◩	Very dark lavender/cranberry	208/603
⊟	Dark lavender/light cranberry	209/604
⊡	Light violet/very light cranberry	554/605
⬚	Dark bright green	699
☒	Light bright green	701
⊡	White	White
■	Black	310

FRIENDLY KITTENS

*S*urprise a cat-lover with this endearing placemat and matching egg warmer. Both are worked from Aida fabric and finished with bright red bias binding. These three friendly little kittens will brighten every meal, and delight any child.

EGG WARMER

Materials

20 x 12 cm piece of 11 count white Aida fabric
Lining 20 x 12 cm piece of white cotton fabric
DMC stranded embroidery cottons in the colours indicated on the colour key on page 91
50 cm of 1 cm wide red bias binding

Finished size 9 x 9.5 cm.
See the General Instructions and Stitch Library on pages 92–6.

Method Trace the pattern for the egg warmer and cut out the paper pattern. Cut the Aida into two equal pieces measuring 10 x 12 cm, and outline the pattern on one piece with running stitches. Following the graph, embroider the motif in cross stitch in the centre of the fabric, 4 cm from the bottom edge. Work each cross over one fabric square, using three strands of embroidery cotton. When the cross stitching is complete, work the outlines in backstitch, using two strands of dark steel grey number 414. Work the mouth in black.

To finish Cut the pattern twice each from Aida and lining fabric, adding a 1.5 cm wide hem on the bottom edge of the Aida pieces. Place the cotton pieces between the Aida pieces, with *wrong sides* together. Fold a 1.5 cm wide hem to the wrong side. Sew all the pieces together with bias binding. Sew a 16 cm piece of bias binding in half across its width. Tie into a bow and sew it onto the top of the egg warmer.

PLACEMAT

Materials

35 x 50 cm piece of 11 count white Aida fabric
DMC stranded embroidery cottons in the colours indicated on the colour key
1.70 m of 1 cm wide red bias binding

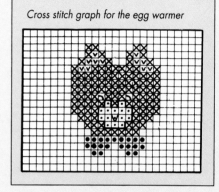

Cross stitch graph for the egg warmer

Pattern (actual size) for the egg warmer

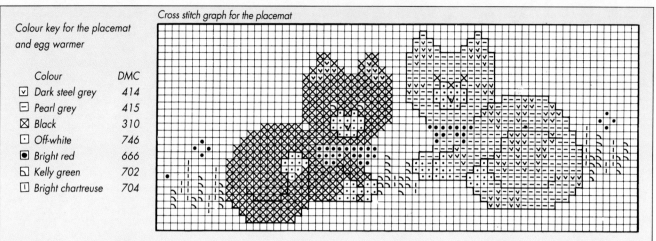

Colour key for the placemat and egg warmer

Colour		DMC
☑	Dark steel grey	414
⊟	Pearl grey	415
⊠	Black	310
⊡	Off-white	746
◉	Bright red	666
◺	Kelly green	702
⊺	Bright chartreuse	704

Cross stitch graph for the placemat

Finished size 35 x 50 cm.
See the General Instructions and Stitch Library on pages 92–6.

Method Round the corners of the Aida fabric and finish the edges with bias binding. Following the graph, embroider the motif in cross stitch in the top left corner. Work each cross over one fabric square, using three strands of embroidery cotton. Start the embroidery with the right lower stitch, 10 cm from the top edge and 22.5 cm from the left side. When the cross stitching is complete, work the outlines in backstitch, using two strands of cotton: use black for the grey cat and dark steel grey number 414 for the black cat. Work the mouths in black.

GENERAL INSTRUCTIONS

INSTRUCTIONS

Always read the instructions for a project right through before starting work. Individual work methods for all projects are fully described and all required graphs, diagrams and stitches are included. Graphs are printed throughout the book; large graphs appear on the special foldout sheets in the centre. If you need to use these sheets, the project directions will give the foldout sheet letter (A–F). Gently ease open the book staples, remove all the sheets together to avoid damaging them, and close the staples again.

FABRICS

All projects state the required type and amount of fabric. Counted work requires the use of a fabric with an even weave, so that the threads may be easily counted as you stitch from the graph. Usually one square on the graph is equal to one stitch. On linen and Davossa this stitch is commonly worked over two threads, on Aida, over one square and on hardanger fabric, over one pair of double threads. Check each project, however, for specific instructions.

Always remove fabric selvedges, as these shrink more than the rest of the fabric during washing and ironing. Always cut the fabrics to be embroidered in a straight line, guided by the fabric weave. To avoid unravelling, work large stitches with basting thread around the fabric edges. Avoid knots on threads, as these cause unattractive lumps on the right side. Always work cross stitches in the same direction: for instance, with the top arm

always from left top to right bottom. For large areas, first embroider a row of half crosses, and complete them on the return journey. Backstitch or outline stitches are embroidered after all the cross stitching is completed. These outlines are usually worked in a shade darker colour than the adjacent cross stitches. Do not carry the thread across long distances at the back, especially when these areas are not covered with stitches, as the threads will show through unattractively on the front of the work.

If you have difficulty obtaining a particular fabric colour, dye a piece of white fabric with Dylon hot-water dye. Always follow the manufacturers directions and test a sample piece fist.

Evenweave fabrics should have the required number of threads to the centimetre. To check this lay the fabric flat, then mark 1 centimetre (or 1 inch, whichever you prefer) with two pins. Count the number of threads between the two pins. This will give you the thread count, which is not necessarily the stitch count of your fabric. The inch equivalents of the metric names of linen (linen 10 has 10 threads to the centimetre) are given here for your guidance.

Linen 8	20 threads to the inch
Linen 10	25 or 26 threads to the inch
Linen 11	28 threads to the inch
Linen 12	30 threads to the inch
Linen 13	32 threads to the inch
Linen 14	35 threads to the inch
Linen 16	40 threads to the inch

Davossa is a 100 per cent cotton fabric suitable for every type of embroidery. It has a thread count of 7 threads to 1 centimetre or 18 threads to the inch.

Hardanger fabric is specially woven in double threads. Hardanger fabric has 9 double threads to 1 centimetre or 22 double threads to the inch.

Aida fabric is specially woven into blocks, to give squares for stitching. Aida is very popular for working counted thread work and comes in a variety of colours. The different Aida fabrics are referred to by the number of squares to the inch; the larger the number the more squares per inch, and so the finer the fabric. Aida is available in 11, 14, 16 and 18 count. Aida is also available in a band, sometimes referred to as **Ribband**. This 14 and 15 count (stitches to the inch) band comes in three different widths, 3 cm, 5 cm and 8 cm and can be purchased in any length. The long edges of the band are already finished, often with a coloured edging.

Herta and **Hertarette** are two Aida style fabrics with fewer squares to the inch.

WASTE CANVAS

Waste canvas is available in embroidery shops and allows you to work counted embroidery on any background fabric that does not have a natural grid for counting. Waste canvas is also available in different counts: 8, 10, 12 and 14 (stitches per inch). Purchase a piece of waste canvas larger than your design. Centre, then tack the canvas in place over the area where the design is to be

stitched. Stitch the design, making sure you work through both layers of fabric. When the stitching is complete, totally dampen your work, then remove the waste canvas threads singly, horizontally and vertically, using a pair of tweezers. You will be left with the cross-stitched design on your fabric.

THREADS

Many types of thread are available for embroidery. The embroidery thread most used is **stranded cotton**, which comes in a skein of approximately 8 metres in length. There are six strands of thread in the skein. Cut the length you require (usually no more than an arm length, otherwise the thread loses its sheen and becomes fluffy), then strand off the desired number of threads. Even if you are going to use all six threads, you should separate them and put them back together for shinier, smoother work. Stranded cotton is popular for counted cross stitch, shadow work, cutwork and crewel embroidery.

Broder cotton (DMC article 107) number 16 and 20 is a non-divisible embroidery thread suitable for all types of embroidery. Number 25 broder cotton is also available, but only in white or ecru, if you prefer to use a finer thread.

NEEDLES AND PINS

For counted work on evenweave fabrics, tapestry needles (those with a blunt end) are used. They come in a variety of sizes, 18, 20 22, 24 and 26, the larger the number the finer the needle. Never leave the needle in your fabric as it will eventually rust and leave a mark that is almost impossible to remove. This rule applies also to pins. Lace pins are suitable for work on good-quality fabrics as they are a very fine sharp pin.

TRANSFERRING DESIGNS

Counted thread work does not require the transfer of the design, as it is worked from graphs.

CLOTHING PATTERNS

No seam allowance is included on the patterns, so a 1 cm wide seam allowance should be added when cutting out fabric pieces, unless patterns instructions direct otherwise.

When measurements only are given for making patterns for straight pieces, always make a pattern from paper first, rather than cut straight into the fabric. The measurements given for straight pieces include seam allowance.

Seams Unless otherwise indicated, sew all pieces together with right sides facing and a 1 cm wide seam. Finish all seams to prevent fraying. Press seams after sewing. When topstitching, press the seam allowance to one side, and topstitch on right side of work.

Gathering Make two rows of long machine stitches either side of the 1 cm seam line. Pull the top gathering threads up and evenly distribute the gathers. Wind the thread ends around a pin in a figure of eight to hold the gathers in place while you are sewing.

SPECIAL TECHNIQUES

Buttonhole loop Make a small stitch to secure at the start and then make two or three stitches as long as the loop is to be. Work close buttonhole stitch, purl edge outwards, over the threads, taking care not to catch the fabric.

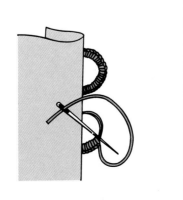

Attaching bias binding Align the raw edge of one side of binding with raw edge of fabric. Stitch (along the foldline of the bias if commercial binding is used). Turn the binding over the fabric edge. Turn bias to wrong side and fold raw edge of bias under and hand sew to stitching line, or machine stitch along edge of binding. (If commercial bias binding is used, stitch the existing fold to the stitching line.)

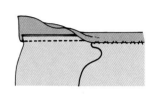

Making and attaching piping Fold a bias strip (without folds) over the cord. Use the zipper foot on a sewing machine to stitch alongside the cord. (The zipper foot allows you to stitch close against the cord.) Position the piping on the fabric, placing the stitchline over the seamline. Place second fabric piece in place, and stitch cord between fabrics, using zipper foot.

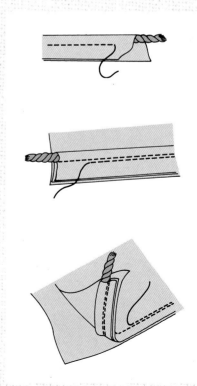

MITRED CORNERS

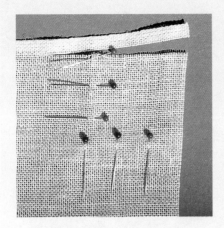

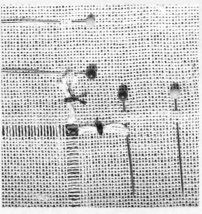

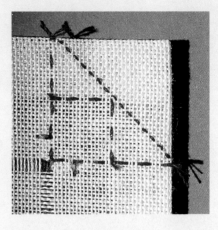

1. Remove the selvedge. Measure the desired width of the hem-turning all around, and mark with a pin. Count the fabric threads from the fabric edge to the pin. Count the same number of threads again, adding one more thread, and mark with a pin (this will form the hem). Repeat this last step once more (here the marked pin will form the line where the hem will be secured).

2. When making an open hem, remove the desired number of threads from corner to corner, inside the last row of pins. For this, cut the thread about 5 cm away from the corners where these threads intersect. Carefully withdraw the remaining 5 cm thread ends, and weave them back into the fabric inside the hem, or secure the edge with a few small stitches. Keeping the wrong side of the fabric uppermost, fold the turning to the wrong side of the fabric, and crease with your thumb-nail.

3. Now fold and crease the hem-fold. Turn the right side of the fabric uppermost. Using running stitches, mark the corners as well as the diagonal line that runs exactly over all the cross-points of the hem-fold.

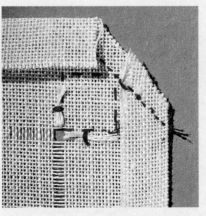

4. With the wrong side of the fabric uppermost, fold the diagonal corner double over its marked line. Trim the corner 0.75 cm underneath the fold.

5. Trim the diagonal corners of the turnings, as shown in the photograph.

6. Refold the hem towards the line where it will be secured, and baste the diagonal corners with a small turning. Close the mitre with small overcast stitches. Baste the hem in place.

STITCH LIBRARY

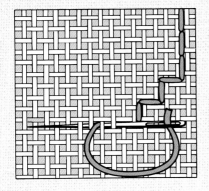

Backstitch

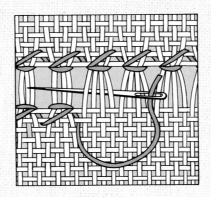

Ladder hemstitch

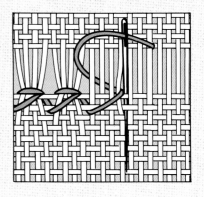

Open hemstitch

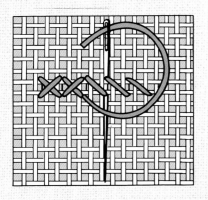

Cross stitch

Star stitch

Basketweave stitch

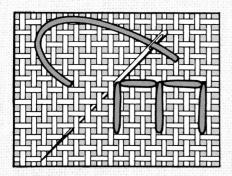

Four-sided edge stitch
1. Work three sides of the stitch at the position of the final hem edge.

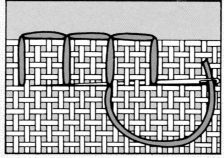

2. Turn the surplus fabric to the wrong side and work the fourth edge of the stitch to hold the hem in place.

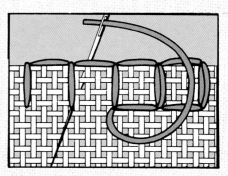

3. The final stitch will form a double thread on the upright arm of the 'box' and a slanted stitch on the back.

Herringbone stitch

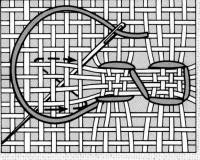

Four-sided stitch

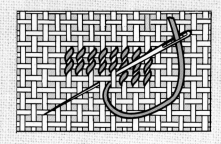

Continental stitch

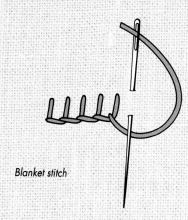

Blanket stitch

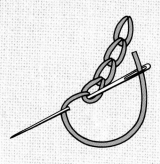

Chain stitch

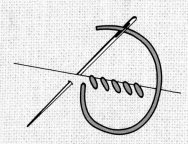

Overcast stitch

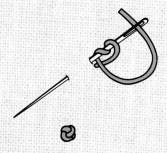

French knot

Published by Murdoch Books®, a division of Murdoch Magazines Pty Ltd, 213 Miller Street, North Sydney NSW 2060

Design: Di Quick
Managing Editor: Christine Eslick
Line drawings: Jan Düttmer
Translation: Marianne Porteners
Cover photography: Joe Filshie
Cover and page 14 styling: Georgina Dolling
Publisher: Anne Wilson
International Sales Director: Mark Newman
General Manager: Mark Smith

National Library of Australia
Cataloguing-in-Publication Data
Cross stitch
ISBN 0 86411 312 9
1. Cross-stitch – Patterns
746.443041

First published 1993. Reprinted 1993, 1996.
Printed by Prestige Litho, Queensland

Acknowledgements
The publisher thanks the following for assistance in the preparation of this book: DMC Myart and Neree Hartog; and Jan Hook and Fiona Hook for cross stitch.
Every effort is made to ensure the availability of materials used in this book, but the availability of particular colours and fabrics cannot be guaranteed.